ROMANS

A Deep Dive Into God's Letter to the Church at Rome

William Ciofani

Twenty Seven Books

Copyright © 2025 William Ciofani

Published by Twenty Seven Books
www.twentysevenbooks.com

Library of Congress Control Number: 2025915274
Printed in the United States of America

All rights reserved. No part of this book may be reproduced, or stored in a retrieval system, or transmitted in any form or by any means, electronic, mechanical, photocopying, recording, or otherwise, without express written permission of the publisher. The only exception is brief quotations in printed reviews.

ISBN: 978-1-968895-00-6

Unless otherwise stated, Scripture quotations are taken from the New American Standard Bible®, Copyright © 1995 by The Lockman Foundation. Used by permission. All rights reserved.

Scripture quotations labeled ESV are from the ESV® Bible (The Holy Bible, English Standard Version®), copyright © 2001 by Crossway, a publishing ministry of Good News Publishers. Used by permission. All rights reserved.

Excerpts from the English translation of the Catechism of the Catholic Church for the United States of America, copyright © 1994, United States Catholic Conference, Inc.–Libreria Editrice Vaticana. Used with permission.

Author photograph by David J. Yanes

Cover design by Twenty Seven Books

CONTENTS

Title Page
Copyright
Introduction
Chapter One — 1
Chapter Two — 14
Chapter Three — 23
Chapter Four — 34
Chapter Five — 45
Chapter Six — 54
Chapter Seven — 65
Chapter Eight — 75
Chapter Nine — 92
Chapter Ten — 104
Chapter Eleven — 113
Chapter Twelve — 124
Chapter Thirteen — 132
Chapter Fourteen — 137
Chapter Fifteen — 145
Chapter Sixteen — 156
About The Author — 163
Loved This Study? — 165

INTRODUCTION

Paul wrote this letter to the church at Rome while in Corinth, around 56–58 AD. At the close of Paul's third missionary journey (Acts 19), just before his departure for Jerusalem, he entrusted this letter to Phoebe, who was setting sail for Rome (Romans 16:1). Tertius, who served as Paul's scribe, assisted in writing this letter (Romans 16:22).

We know that Jews from Rome were present in Jerusalem on the day of Pentecost. Since many of them responded to the gospel (Acts 2:10), there must have been a church in Rome long before either Paul or Peter arrived.

After leaving Corinth, Paul was arrested upon his eventual arrival in Jerusalem (Acts 21:33). From there, he traveled to Rome by way of Caesarea under Roman custody (Acts 23:23–28:14), where he was kept under house arrest for about three years. During this period, Paul wrote letters to the Ephesians, Philippians, Colossians, and Philemon. About eight years after writing this letter, Paul was martyred in Rome.

CHAPTER ONE

The importance of the gospel, what it reveals, and why it is needed.

Verses 1–5

Paul identifies himself and immediately points to Jesus Christ, the subject of this letter. As you read these verses, notice how Paul states that he has one mission, one message, and one result for those who receive the message.

1) Read Romans 1:1–3

    a) Verse 1: How did Paul describe himself?

    b) Verse 1: What was his mission?

    c) Verse 2: Where was the gospel revealed?

    d) Verse 3: Who is the gospel concerning?

    e) Verse 3: What two facts are we told about His lineage?

Paul was considered an apostle because he had seen the risen Jesus (1 Corinthians 9:1), but notice how Paul also states he was a servant set apart to proclaim the gospel.

What is the gospel? It is good news from God to a dying world concerning the promise of the Messiah who would not only save those in the world (John 3:17, 12:47), but also free a people from their sins (Matthew 1:21). The gospel is good news for everyone (Luke 2:10; Acts 8:12) with the result being salvation and joy for those who receive and place their faith in it.

What isn't the gospel? It is not a promise that requires works as a qualification (Ephesians 2:8–9). This truth will be clearly revealed in this letter.

What is the gospel about? Jesus and no one else! It is not about a specific church or any other individual, only about Jesus Christ. Jesus was born a descendant of David, just as was prophesied in many places (2 Samuel 7:12-13; Psalm 89:3–4; Isaiah 11:1–5). Mary (Luke 3) and Joseph (Matthew 1) were also from the family of David.

Did the gospel just come to light during the time of Jesus? Exactly when and where was it revealed? Understand that it was revealed throughout the Old Testament as God slowly revealed facts about His Son, the Messiah, who has fulfilled over four hundred prophecies from the Old Testament.

For example:

- Abraham was told the Messiah would be his descendant (Genesis 12:2–3) through his son Isaac (Genesis 17:19).

- Balaam revealed that the Messiah would be a descendant of Isaac's son Jacob (Numbers 24:17).

- Jacob prophesied that the Messiah would be from the tribe of Judah (Genesis 49:10).

- Isaiah foretold that the Messiah would come from the family of Jesse, David's father (Isaiah 11:10).

- Isaiah emphasized the Messiah would be God (Isaiah 7:14, 9:6).

- God promised David that the Messiah would be one of his descendants (1 Chronicles 17:11–14).

- Daniel was told when the Messiah would come (Daniel 9:25).

- Micah foretold where the Messiah would be born (Micah 5:2).

- Isaiah foretold of the miracles Jesus would perform (Isaiah 35:5–6).

- Isaiah foretold how the Messiah would be rejected by the Jews (Isaiah 8:14, 49:7).

- Isaiah foretold that Messiah would come for both the Jews and Gentiles (Isaiah 28:16, 11:10, 63:16).

- Isaiah foretold why the Messiah would die (Isaiah 53).

- David said the Messiah would be raised from the dead (Psalm 16:10).

- Jeremiah (Jeremiah 31:31–34) and Ezekiel (Ezekiel 36:25-27) spoke of a new covenant that the Messiah would bring.

2) Read Romans 1:4–5

a) Verse 4: Who is Jesus declared as?

b) Verse 4: What event revealed His power?

c) Verse 5: What did Paul receive from Jesus?

d) Verse 5: What is the purpose of Paul's commission?

Jesus was both God and man, as He had the nature of the flesh (John 1:14) and the Spirit of holiness. No one can rightfully question Jesus's divinity, which was demonstrated and proved by His resurrection (Matthew 12:39–40; Acts 13:29–35). While Jesus was always the Son of God (John 17:5), He was also declared so by His resurrection! The miracles He performed and the fact that He returned from the dead prove His deity and that He is also the Messiah.

Notice how Paul states that he received grace and apostleship. This letter will expound on the grace that God bestows on everyone. Every good thing that a believer receives (both Gentile and Jew) comes from Jesus (James 1:17). Paul makes it clear that it is only through Jesus that one can obtain grace and truth (John 1:17). This includes the power to be obedient to the faith (Romans 16:26). Why? Both for His name's sake and so He will be glorified.

What is "obedience to the faith?" Believing in the gospel of Jesus and living your life to bring Him glory. This includes obedience to Him (Acts 6:7). The faith also refers to the written body of apostolic teaching inspired by the Holy Spirit (1 Timothy 3:9, 3:13, 4:6; Jude 1:3).

While God commands that everyone should repent (Acts 17:30–31) and believe in Christ (1 John 3:23; John 6:29), no one is able to obey God without the grace that He gives. Christians are actually granted repentance (Acts 5:31, 11:18). Notice how Paul does not refer to obedience to the Law, but rather to the faith (Mark 1:15). Why? Because Christians are dead to God's Law, a truth Paul will discuss in the coming chapters.

Verses 6–7

Paul defines to whom he is writing and who they are in Christ.

3) Read Romans 1:6–7

a) Verse 6: How does Paul describe the recipients of this letter?

b) Verse 7: How else does Paul describe the believers in Rome?

c) Verse 7: What blessing does Paul proclaim on those who read this letter?

Paul encouraged the recipients of this letter that they were also included in the gospel, not differentiating between slaves or free, but rather all Christians in Rome. While only a few men were called apostles, all believers are described as loved by God and called saints (Jude 1; Revelation 17:14). The only biblical qualification for a saint is being a genuine believer in Jesus Christ. Just as Paul does in most of his epistles, he blesses the recipients of this letter with a salutation of grace and peace from both God and Jesus (1 Corinthians 1:3; Galatians 1:3; Ephesians 1:2).

The fact that Jesus is mentioned with the Father further confirms His deity. The grace that Christians receive is what enables them to have peace with God (Romans 5:1). While all believers have received both grace and peace from the Father through Jesus Christ, it can be multiplied through the knowledge of God and the Lord Jesus Christ (2 Peter 1:2).

◆ ◆ ◆

Verses 8–12

Paul discusses his desire and purpose for coming to Rome.

4) Read Romans 1:8–10

a) Verse 8: How does Paul pray to the Father?

b) Verse 8: What was Paul thankful for?

c) Verse 9: Whom did Paul say that he served?

d) Verse 9: Whom did Paul pray for?

e) Verse 10: What did Paul ask God for?

f) Verse 10: What desire did Paul balance his prayer with?

Notice how Paul prayed to the Father through Jesus Christ, who stated that it was only possible to approach the Father through Him (John 14:6; 1 Timothy 2:5). Paul was thankful that since Rome was the capital of the empire, the presence of believers meant that anyone traveling from there would have heard about Christianity. This resulted in Jesus being mentioned throughout the world.

Paul stated how he served God by preaching the gospel of Jesus Christ. Know that you are not serving God if your gospel includes anyone besides Jesus. It is not Jesus and His mother; it is not Jesus and any saint; it is not Jesus and works. The gospel is about Jesus alone as God shares His glory with no one else (Isaiah 42:8, 48:11).

Many times, the power of prayer is overlooked. Notice how Paul prayed unceasingly for those in Rome (Ephesians 6:18; 1 Thessalonians 5:17). The real fact is that most, if not all, opportunities to serve God result from His will (Ephesians 2:10). Paul understood the sovereignty of God and balanced his prayerful desire to get to Rome by also praying God's will.

5) Read Romans 1:11–12

a) Verse 11: What did Paul want to give to those in Rome?

b) Verse 11: What would the result be?

c) Verse 12: How did Paul balance that statement?

Paul longed to see those in Rome as he felt that God would allow him to impart a spiritual gift or gifts to them (Acts 19:21). Incidentally, this shows how Peter was not the bishop at Rome, as there would have been no need for Paul to do so if Peter was present there. Paul's humility is revealed by mentioning how (just like all Christians) he needed to be encouraged. Christians are encouraged by hearing testimonies from fellow believers in the Lord and witnessing the power of their faith.

❖ ❖ ❖

Verses 13–16

Paul now tells how the key to bearing fruit is the gospel.

6) Read Romans 1:13–15

a) Verse 13: What had Paul planned on doing?

b) Verse 13: What had he hoped to obtain?

c) Verse 13: Among what group of people?

d) Verse 14: To whom is Paul obliged to give the gospel?

e) Verse 15: What was Paul anxious to give to those in Rome?

Acts informs us that Claudius expelled all the Jews from Rome (Acts 18:2). This would have happened about 50 AD and was one obstacle preventing Paul from reaching Rome. Due to the absence of Jews, the Roman church at this time likely consisted mostly of Gentiles. When Paul stated that he was under obligation to both Greeks and barbarians, he differentiated between Gentiles who spoke Greek and those who didn't. The Greek language was used by the educated of the Roman Empire.

Paul knew that both his life mission (Romans 1:1) and the Great Commission (Mark 16:15) included giving the message of the gospel to everyone. He also knew that he was an apostle to the Gentiles, while Peter was the apostle to the Jews (Galatians 2:7-8).

The world is sick, and the gospel is the cure. This gospel was God's plan from all eternity (Romans 16:25–26). Wouldn't it be great if every Christian (just as Paul) experienced such a sense of gratitude that they felt not only compelled (1 Corinthians 9:16; Romans 1:14), but also eager to share the gospel with everyone as the Lord gave them the opportunity (Romans 1:15). Paul was not only always eager to preach the gospel, but also to die for it (Acts 21:13; 2 Timothy 4:6).

7) Read Romans 1:16

a) What is Paul not ashamed of?

b) How is the gospel described?

c) What is necessary for salvation?

d) Who is the gospel for?

Here was simple Paul, alone and without weapons, ready to preach the gospel to those in Rome. Little did he know he would come as a prisoner (Acts 28:16).

Did Paul go to Rome alone? No! One is never alone when one serves the Lord of Lords and King of Kings.

What weapon did Paul plan on bringing? Only the dynamite gospel about a crucified Jewish man who happens to be the Messiah and Savior of the world.

Paul accepted his role to suffer greatly for his gospel preaching (Acts 14:19, 16:23, 17:10) because he knew the gospel is what God uses to save people. Paul knew that the key to obtaining fruit among the Gentiles was giving the gospel, as he understood that the actual Word of God is what saves (1 Corinthians 1:18).

Paul knew the gospel brings genuine faith that results in obedience. It is not our intellect or the creative way we witness, but rather the power of the Word of God that saves and delivers those who place their faith in it, rescued from the things this letter will soon discuss. Most feel inadequate when witnessing or preaching, failing to realize that the power is in the Word of God. Those in Rome would especially appreciate this verse, as power was very important to them and something that Romans typically boasted about.

Paul states that putting your faith in the gospel is necessary for salvation. This includes what the Old Testament revealed about the coming Messiah. Things like His life, death, and resurrection (2 Timothy 2:8). Again, notice how he does not mention works as necessary for salvation, as they are not part of the gospel, which is all about faith. This was revealed by the miracles Jesus performed in response to faith, not works (Matthew 9:22, 9:29, 15:28; Mark 10:52).

Notice how God uses the word *'salvation.'* This term comes from the Greek word *soteria*, which means *'deliverance.'* But deliverance from what? Sin and death. Man must be delivered from the horrid effects of sin, one of which is death (Ezekiel 18:4). While the gospel is about a crucified Jewish man who happens to be the Savior of the world, it is for both Jews and Gentiles. It first came to the Jews, who then brought it to the Gentiles (Matthew 28:19).

Verse 17

Paul defines exactly what the gospel reveals.

8) Read Romans 1:17

a) What is revealed in the gospel?

b) How is it available?

c) What enables those who believe to have salvation?

David knew and told of the gospel when he stated that the Lord would deliver him with His own righteousness (Psalm 31:1). Paul now begins to expound on exactly how this is accomplished. The most overlooked part of the gospel of Jesus Christ is that God's righteousness is revealed in it. How? All are shown to be sinners while Christ lived a sin-free life, thereby earning and providing righteousness for those who put their faith in Him.

The gospel reveals how this righteousness is only available by faith. People receive God's righteousness when they put their faith in the gospel that states that they have no righteousness of their own and are in need of the righteousness of God. Thus, the righteous live by faith (Habakkuk 2:4; Galatians 3:11).

The righteous are saved and live by faith. After coming to faith, by an act of faith in the gospel, one receives God's righteousness. In fact, 2 Corinthians 5:21 (ESV) tells us, "For our sake he made him to be sin who knew no sin, so that in him we might become the righteousness of God." This salvation is not by works of the Law (Romans 11:6). Christians then preach the gospel by faith, which brings faith to the one who receives it.

Why are many people unaware of the simple truth about God's righteousness? One answer is that it is only revealed in the gospel they reject. Another answer is that people fail to accept and acknowledge that they are unrighteous (Matthew 9:12; Luke 5:31) and have no righteousness to contribute to their salvation.

❖ ❖ ❖

Verses 18–23

Why the gospel (which reveals God's righteousness) is needed.

9) Read Romans 1:18

a) What aspect of God's divine nature is also revealed in the gospel?

b) What two things is it turned against?

c) What causes men to suppress the truth?

Besides revealing the righteousness of God, the gospel also reveals why it is needed. The Old Testament reveals the wrath of God toward sin. For instance, Adam and Eve faced the consequences of their rebellion. The flood destroyed the evil world (Genesis 8). Those in Sodom and Gomorrah paid the price for their sin (Genesis 19). The Jews had to wander in the wilderness for forty years due to their sin of rebellion (Numbers 14). Both Israel and Judah were ultimately banished from the Promised Land and to captivity due to their sin (2 Kings 17; 2 Kings 25).

The Word of God describes sin as both ungodliness and unrighteousness. The sin of ungodliness is turning away from the one true God (Yahweh) to other so-called gods. This ungodliness results in all forms of unrighteousness, which is not only sinning against the one true God but also toward other human beings.

Most, if not all, unrighteousness is a derivative of not trusting that God alone is sufficient for every need. Notice how unrighteousness suppresses the truth that people know about God. Even though they know the truth, many refuse to acknowledge or apply it in their lives. You might wonder how this is done today. With lies like: there is no God, there are many gods, there is no hell, there is no judgment, and that all roads lead to God.

We are warned that God's righteousness is needed because the gospel reveals His wrath toward sin. This is a huge part of the gospel that is usually left out. This important fact is revealed over and over in the Old Testament. Because God is righteous, He could not disregard or overlook man's sin. His Word states that the soul who sins must die (Ezekiel 18:4), so a righteous God came up with a righteous answer, that is, Jesus, living a sin-free life and paying the price for everyone's sin. God solved within Himself the huge problem that was created by our sins.

10) Read Romans 1:19–20

a) Verse 19: What is plain to every person?

b) Verse 19: Why?

c) Verse 20: What does creation reveal about God?

d) Verse 20: What is the result for everyone?

Creation bears witness to its Creator (Psalm 19:1). God has revealed His existence through the things He has made. Man is without excuse because everyone has enough intelligence to discern that there has to be a Creator. How? Through nature's wonder, which confirms this truth (Psalm 8:1).

What does nature reveal? God's eternal power and His divine nature as the Designer (Job 12:7–9). Since God is the Creator, He must logically be eternal.

11) Read Romans 1:21

a) What two things did man fail to do despite knowing (being aware of) God?

b) What is the result of rejecting the Creator?

God has created everything for His glory (Psalm 148). This includes all of mankind (Psalm 29:1; 1 Chronicles 16:28–29). Adam and Eve (Genesis 3:8) and Cain and Abel (Genesis 4:4–6) had fellowship with God. It was not until after the birth of Seth's son Enosh (Genesis 4:26) that men began to "call on the Lord." Methuselah lived to nine hundred sixty-nine years of age (the oldest age man ever lived) (Genesis 5:21). His life overlapped Adam's by two hundred forty-three years. Methuselah died in the year of the flood. This means that until the flood, mankind would have had someone who would have heard or known firsthand Adam's account of creation.

While nature reveals much about God, it does not reveal His personal character traits. His holiness, patience, and righteousness are not revealed in nature. Nature also does not reveal that He is love, light, and truth. These are things revealed in the gospel Paul refers to and only found in God's Word. Know that nature alone does not reveal the gospel Paul refers to and about which he will now expound.

What did the people do with what they were revealed? Even though they knew about God, they did not honor or give thanks to Him. Their sin caused them to turn from the truth they knew to false gods. Their heart was darkened. God's Word tells how the Jews had fallen to the place where they credited their blessings to the pagan gods they worshiped (Hosea 2:5; Jeremiah 44:17–18). Even today, people suppress the truth, resulting in a false peace that they won't have to answer to God for their sins (Psalm 10:4).

Note the widespread lack of gratitude toward God for His faithfulness and grace. People today reject this truth by embracing doctrines like evolution. The result of rejecting God's mercy is a hardened heart. The sin of Pharaoh caused him to have a hardened heart (Exodus 7:13), leading to God Himself further hardening it for His glory (Exodus 10:1–2). Because mankind is not able to clean his own darkened heart (Proverbs 20:9), God gives a new heart to believers as a result of responding in faith to the gospel (Ezekiel 36:26).

12) Read Romans 1:22–23

a) Verse 22: What do those who reject God think of themselves?

b) Verse 22: What does God call those who fail to acknowledge Him?

c) Verse 23: What did those who reject Him end up doing?

With the overwhelming evidence for a Creator, only a fool would state that there is no God (Psalm 14:1, 53:1). Those who reject the one true God normally turn to a substitute invented by someone considered wise by the masses. Paul had previously seen the images of gods (probably statues) in Greece, where he had earlier been. In Athens, he even noticed an altar to the unknown god (Acts 17:23), which he used as an opening for the gospel. In Ephesus, Paul would have witnessed an image that people thought fell from heaven to the temple of Artemis (Acts 19:35).

The Egyptians depicted gods as animals, birds, cows, and frogs. The Canaanites had Baal and Ashtoreth. The Ammonites worshipped Molech by sacrificing their children to him. The Moabites had Chemosh. The Babylonians and Assyrians had the goddess Ishtar. The Greeks had gods like Zeus and Diana. God told the Jews that there was no other God (Deuteronomy 32:39), and they still turned from Him to other false gods (Psalm 106:19–21). Their persistent idolatry was utter foolishness.

Verses 24–28

God's response to man's rejection of Him and the result.

13) Read Romans 1:24–28

    a) Verses 24 & 26: How did God react to man's rejection of Him?

    b) Verse 25: What did man exchange the truth of God for?

    c) Verse 25: Whom did the people then choose to worship?

    d) Verses 26 & 27: What sin is mentioned as "unnatural?"

    e) Verse 27: What did the people receive as a result of this sin?

    f) Verse 28: Exactly why did God give them over to their lust?

God's wrath toward those who rejected Him included no longer restraining people from their idolatry, with the end resulting in gross immorality and the consequences it brings. In the past, God said He would allow false prophets to perform signs as a way to test the people (Deuteronomy 13:1–4). When they fail the test, He gives them over to their lust, so they believe a lie. The prophet Isaiah tells how the Lord has sealed the eyes and hearts of the non-believing (Isaiah 44:18).

We see this everywhere in our culture today—willful blindness and hard-heartedness. And God will soon do so again in the tribulation period when those who rejected Him are sent a deluding influence so they will believe a lie (2 Thessalonians 2:11–12). Because God is truth, anything about Him and not from Him is a lie. He told the prophet Jeremiah that Judah was being judged because they turned from Him to a lie (Jeremiah 13:25). Know that all lies originate from Satan, whom Jesus described as the father of lies (John 8:44). Adam and Eve were deceived with the original lie that they could become like God (Genesis

3:5).

All of creation is for the glory of its Creator, Jesus Christ (1 Chronicles 29:11; Psalm 145:11). Man has rejected God and turned to the doctrine of the devil, inciting attention to something other than the true God of creation, who is worthy of all praise and glory. Those who are told to worship Mary and the saints are being taught to worship the creation rather than the Creator.

Without a holy God to answer to, man feels the freedom to do whatever he wants. It is normal for a man to worship his Creator, but man deviated from what is natural, so God allowed deviances like homosexuality, which itself is against anything natural. The result is receiving the penalty for their sin. Keep in mind that at the time this letter was written, homosexuality was rampant in the Roman Empire. It is important to be clear that God is condemning homosexuality here as something both sinful and abnormal (Leviticus 20:13; Deuteronomy 22:5). Let me again repeat this important point: mankind's failure to acknowledge God resulted in being given over to a depraved mind, which is the source of human sinful actions.

❖ ❖ ❖

Verses 29–32

Mankind's state of wickedness.

14) Read Romans 1:29–32

a) Verse 29: What are those who reject God filled with?

b) Verses 29-31: How are these people described?

c) Verse 32: What are these people aware of?

d) Verse 32: What do they do despite this knowledge?

The result of being given over to a depraved mind is the inability to discern right from wrong and the bent to choose wrong. This caused mankind to decline into greater wickedness. While Paul is very clear as to the evilness of the unnatural sin of homosexuality (Romans 1:26–27), he also lists many other sins (covetousness, malice, envy, murder, strife, deceit, and maliciousness). These depraved sinners are described as being without understanding and haters of God. Notice how the result for these people is not only committing these sins but promoting them.

❖ ❖ ❖

Romans Chapter One gives us an overview of the downward spiral that mankind experienced. In the beginning, man had fellowship with God. Creation itself reveals the presence of an eternal God. Man rejected this truth, forming religions that turned to ridiculous idols. Man went from having knowledge about his Creator to foolish speculations.

Due to His righteousness, God responded to these sins by giving people up to their lusts, which led to the further darkening of their hearts. The result was a decayed creation separated from God and being so lost and full of unrighteousness that it encouraged giving in to sinful desires. This chapter has shown how those without the Law (Gentiles) are guilty before a perfect God. This sets the stage for the next chapter, which will reveal how those with the Law (Jews) are also just as guilty.

CHAPTER TWO

The Jews who had the Law and circumcision are also guilty before God.

Paul now directs his attention from those who had rejected what creation had clearly shown, resulting in man-made religion (idolatry), to the Jewish people who had rejected the God who not only led them (Isaiah 63:11) but who was also visibly present in the Temple (2 Chronicles 7:1–2), the very place that the Law required all adult Jewish men to visit three times a year (Deuteronomy 16:16).

❖ ❖ ❖

Verses 1–3

Paul now talks about the unrighteousness of the Jews who had not only looked down on the Gentiles as being without hope, but also condemned them for their sins.

1) Read Romans 2:1–3

    a) Verse 1: Who is without excuse?

    b) Verse 2: What are we told about God's judgment

    c) Verses 1 & 2: What happens when you judge another and then do the same thing?

    d) Verse 3: What truth does Paul remind the Jews of?

Paul now directs the discussion to those who believe they were free from God's future judgment and wrath because they had not indulged in the sins previously mentioned (Romans 1:29–31). Think of it as someone saying, "I am not that bad." Notice how he uses the word "therefore" to make the point that the recipients of the letter were guilty of those sins. Keep in mind that while not every person has committed all the sins previously mentioned, everyone has committed most of them.

Trusting God should include trusting His righteous judgment on sinners; He does not need our help. The error most make concerning judgment is not realizing that God's standard is perfection. Don't judge if you are not perfect (Matthew 7:3–5). Jesus used the Pharisees as an example of the hypocrisy discussed here (Matthew 23:2–3; Luke 18:10–14).

It is very easy to judge others because sins always look worse when others commit them. The fact is, condemning another for something you practice can bring a judgment on yourself (Matthew 7:1–2; Luke 6:37). Paul again reminds the Jews that it is the righteousness of God that causes Him to have wrath toward all sin, including self-righteousness (Romans 1:17). Paul earlier told of the wrath of God. He now reinforces his point concerning unrighteousness by telling of God's judgment of sinners. Because the Old Testament reveals God's judgment for the sins of the Jewish nation, the Jewish people should have clearly understood that their election as God's chosen people did not preclude them from judgment.

By reminding the Jews of their self-righteousness, Paul is reinforcing the truth of the unrighteousness of everyone (both Jew and Gentile). It is interesting to point out that this letter was written to those at the Church of Rome, and the subject mentioned here is self-righteousness. This is the very institution that today claims the very thing that the Jews are being condemned for, by stating that its leaders are the holiest people on this earth. This viewpoint is affirmed in the Catechism, which states, "The structure of the church is totally ordered to the holiness of Christ's members" (Catechism 773).

Verses 4-11

Paul now describes the blessings bestowed on the nation of Israel and the responsibilities that come with them.

2) Read Romans 2:4-6

a) Verse 4: What had the Jews overlooked?

b) Verse 4: What brings you to repentance?

c) Verse 5: What prevents repentance?

d) Verse 5: What is the result of rejecting the gospel of Jesus Christ?

e) Verse 5: When will this happen?

f) Verse 5: What will God's judgment reveal?

g) Verse 6: What will be the result of God's judgment?

We are told how the self-righteous who judge others think lightly of the mercy of God. Instead of feeling superior, they should be humble (Philippians 2:3). While the Old Testament reveals God's wrath toward sin, it much more reveals His patience and kindness toward a people who had rejected Him (Isaiah 65:2). Many people misinterpret the patience of God, resulting in self-righteousness (Exodus 34:6). This patience was revealed during the time of Noah (1 Peter 3:20). God's patience is what leads one to repentance (2 Peter 3:9) and also, reveals His mercy (Romans 9:23).

Many times, Christians look down on non-believers, not realizing that God's mercy and grace have brought them out of the darkness that they judge others for being in. The real fact is that non-Christians should be loved and shown the same mercy and gentleness that the loving God of the Bible has shown them (Matthew 5:44–45). This reveals God's true character and love, which states that it is His desire that none should perish (2 Peter 3:9).

While God used a different standard when judging angels (who did not get a second chance), His patience and kindness toward wicked men are continually exhibited. This fact needs to be balanced with the truth that not experiencing immediate judgment for sin can encourage individuals into sinning more (Ecclesiastes 8:11). God also warns those who do not yet see the consequences of their sins against making the mistake of thinking that they are getting away with them (Deuteronomy 29:19–20).

Those whose stubbornness prevents them from accepting the truth about God that is present within them and the mercy extended through the gospel of Jesus Christ are storing up wrath in the coming judgment before Him (Revelation 20:11–15). This judgment will be impartial and also revealed as righteous (Proverbs 24:12; Matthew 16:27). While those who accept God's gift of salvation will stand in a different bema judgment before Him (2 Corinthians 5:10), they, too, will have to account for their every deed.

3) Read Romans 2:7–11

a) Verses 7 & 10: How are believers described?

b) Verses 7 & 10: What is their ultimate reward?

c) Verse 8: How are non-believers described?

d) Verses 8 & 9: What is their ultimate reward?

e) Verse 11: What are we told about God's future judgment?

While only genuine Christians will persevere until the end (Luke 8:15; Hebrews 10:36), know that eternal life is a gift (Ephesians 2:8–9). Unlike Christians who typically seek the things above (Romans 8:5; Colossians 3:2), non-believers are described as selfishly ambitious (2 Corinthians 12:20; Galatians 5:20), disobedient and obeying unrighteousness (2 Thessalonians 2:12). Paul will soon discuss how only believers can obey the truth as God has granted them repentance which includes a different relationship to sin than non-believers have (Acts 11:18; 2 Timothy 2:25).

Know that eternal life is in no way a reward for living a good life, as perfection is needed (Deuteronomy 27:26; Matthew 5:48). All of man's deeds done in trying to establish righteousness are, in fact, filthy rags before God (Isaiah 64:6). In continuing his argument against self-righteousness, Paul will soon show how all are sinners in need of a Savior.

We are again told how God's judgment will be perfect and impartial (Deuteronomy 10:17; Acts 10:34; Galatians 2:6). This news might shock the Jews who boasted in the Law and thought of themselves as special before God, thinking He would judge them with a different standard than the Gentiles. The truth is that while God is impartial, He expects more from those to whom He has given more (Luke 12:48).

◆ ◆ ◆

Verses 12–16

God's Law and judgment.

4) Read Romans 2:12–13

a) Verse 12: What are we told about the Gentiles who did not have the Law?

b) Verse 12: What are we told about the Jews who had the Law?

c) Verse 13: What is needed in order to be justified?

Paul now deals with both the Jews who thought they were safe because they had the Law and the Gentiles who might have thought they were safe because they didn't have the Law. We are shown the effect of sin on mankind as it brings eternal death (Ezekiel 18:4). It matters not whether one has or does not have the Law; their sin will be judged. The fact that people died before God gave the Law (around 1449 BC) confirms they were guilty before God.

Most Jews would have thought that having the Law somehow made them better than the Gentiles. They did not realize that the Law they had put their hope in would be the standard used in their judgment (John 5:45). Know that the Law had no provisions for eternal life, as it was a covenant of blessings for obedience and curses for disobedience (Deuteronomy 27:26).

Paul tells the Jews that simply having and hearing the Law is not good enough; obedience is needed. Keep in mind that this is not simply partial obedience; God means perfection (Galatians 3:11). Many so-called Christian religions mistakenly teach that keeping the Law is necessary for eternal life, leaving out the fact that this is impossible because perfection is needed. Christians will naturally obey God and, through Jesus, have fulfilled the requirement of the Law (Romans 8:4). Paul begins to explain why the Gentiles can be judged without the Law.

5) Read Romans 2:14–16

a) Verse 14: What do the Gentiles try to do despite not having the Law?

b) Verse 15: Why are the Gentiles aware of right and wrong?

c) Verse 15: How does this affect their conscience?

d) Verse 16: What does Paul state is part of the gospel

e) Verse 16: Who will judge?

God has assured that no one can claim ignorance of the knowledge between right and wrong, as the work of the Law is written on every heart. Paul earlier told how nature revealed to the Gentiles that there was a Creator (Romans 1:20); he now tells how it is natural that they also have a conscience that will accuse them when they sin. This is why most false Gentile religions include sacrifices of some type. Through the Law, God has ensured everyone has a clear knowledge of their sinfulness. This is a truth that has been distorted into a belief that God will only judge major sins and somehow overlook minor ones.

Paul then reminds the readers how there is a coming judgment of both Jew and Gentile (Acts 24:25) when Jesus will use the Law to judge every sin (Acts 10:42, 17:31). This will be a time when the Father through Jesus will not only judge secret sins (Ecclesiastes 12:14) but also the motivation behind one's actions (1 Corinthians 4:5). Paul again makes it clear that this judgment is a part of the gospel of Jesus Christ (Acts 24:25). That is why salvation is needed (Romans 1:16).

How is the knowledge of coming judgement good news? The knowledge of depravity and coming judgment reveals the need for a Savior. Rejecting God's truth that the wage of any sin is death (Romans 6:23), the Catholic religion wrongly teaches that there are two different types of sins: mortal and venial. Mortal sins result in complete loss of grace (Catechism 1861), while venial sins are lesser sins that do not have the same consequences (Catechism 1863). The invented Purgatory is a place where one pays for their venial sins, while the major ones can only be removed through the sacrament of confession.

◆ ◆ ◆

Verses 17–24

The self-righteous Jews are also guilty before God.

6) Read Romans 2:17–20

a) Verse 17: What might cause the Jews to be arrogant?

b) Verse 17: What did they boast about?

c) Verse 17: What did the Jews rely on?

d) Verse 18: What did the Jews know?

e) Verses 19 & 20: What were they confident of?

f) Verse 20: What does the Law include?

God now warns the Jews who thought they were righteous because they both had and tried to obey the Law. They did not recognize that having the Law is insufficient, as total obedience is needed. Just as Paul had earlier chastised the Jews (Romans 1:18–32), he now continues to tell them that their religion is external. Jesus revealed this when describing the Pharisees as blind guides (Matthew 23:24) who saw themselves as righteous (Luke 18:9–11). Paul had already told of the importance of obedience (Romans 2:13). Keep in mind that the Biblical history of the nation of Israel shows an almost complete disregard for God and His Laws.

The Catholic Church wrongly relies on the Law by teaching that one must obey the commandments if they are to have any chance to enter into heaven (Catechism 2068). While this teaching sounds correct, Paul will soon discuss how it is a gospel of no hope. Just like those taught by the Catholic Church, the Jews were placing their hope on the Law, which only condemned them (John 5:45). They also erroneously thought that the Law only belonged to them.

They had the distorted view that simply having the Law somehow established their righteousness, not knowing that it, in fact, established their unrighteousness. Religion does not teach this truth. Instead, it encourages and teaches its followers to continue trying to obey the Law, as if they might do it right, though again, it is impossible for sinners.

The gospel of Jesus Christ says no, there is a better way! The Jews also thought that being chosen by God meant they would not have to face the same judgment as the Gentiles. Paul chastised them for boasting that they were God's chosen people when they should have glorified God for His righteousness. While they professed God, their actions spoke otherwise. The Jews were confident that the Gentiles were in spiritual darkness. Paul had dealt with this earlier by making the case that while the Jews did have the Law, the Gentiles also had it written on their hearts (Romans 2:15).

Paul is writing this to convince the Jews that what they have needs to be replaced with something real and better. The truth is they did not have what they thought they had and, in fact, only pretended to have it. We will soon discuss how the Law was meant to be only a tutor to lead us to Christ (Galatians 3:24).

7) Read Romans 2:21–24

    a) Verses 21 & 22: What examples of hypocrisy are given?

    b) Verse 23: What did the Jews boast about?

    c) Verses 23 & 24: What was the result of their hypocrisy?

Even today, many so-called Christian leaders teach others what to do but fail to obey God themselves. While teachers will suffer a stricter judgment (James 3:1), hypocrites will suffer greater condemnation (Matthew 23:14). Most people who steal typically reveal that money is an idol in their lives. While the history of the nation of Israel shows that the people continually sought after pagan idols before their captivity, they rejected these practices after their return and became known for their monotheism.

Notice how Paul reminds the Jews how they did not keep the Law. While the Jewish nation boasted in the Law, their hearts were far from God. Today, many so-called Christian religions honor Christ in name only. Many people go to church, leave, and forget about God until the following week. The prophet Ezekiel described how the dispersed Jewish people profaned God's name by their actions (Ezekiel 36:20), which allowed their captors to blaspheme His name as inferior to their gods (Isaiah 52:5). He also tells of how much the God of the Bible cares about His holy name (Ezekiel 36:21).

How many times have you heard Christianity ridiculed because of the way many so-called religious people act? It is even worse when the leaders of the religion are shown to be evil. This causes the name of Jesus to be blasphemed. All of this should come as no surprise, as God warns how Satan will come disguised as a holy person (2 Corinthians 11:14).

❖ ❖ ❖

Verses 25–29

Paul now chastises those who trusted in an outward sign for their relationship with God and tells of something much more profound.

8) Read Romans 2:25–29

a) Verse 25: What might a typical Jewish defense be?

b) Verse 25: What happens if found to be a transgressor of the Law?

c) Verse 26: What if a Gentile obeys the Law?

d) Verse 26: What does this show about the circumcision of the flesh?

e) Verse 27: How will a non-believing Jew feel compared to a Gentile believer?

f) Verse 28: How valuable is outward circumcision?

g) Verse 28 & 29: What type of circumcision is important?

h) Verse 29: By Whom is it performed?

After hearing of the inadequacy of the Law, a Jew now might bring up circumcision as something that also sets them apart. Just as some believe that infant baptism somehow ensures their salvation, the Jews trusted in circumcision (Genesis 17:11) as a rite that equated to sure acceptance by God (Ephesians 2:11). All this because they would inherit the promises that He had made to Abraham.

Paul is now talking about something far greater than the circumcision of the flesh. The Jews failed to realize that while Ishmael was also circumcised (Genesis 17:25), he would not inherit the promises that would only come through Isaac. Jesus told of the requirement of being born from above (John 3:3). Know that this does not happen when baptized with a water baptism, but rather a commitment of one's faith in Him.

Paul is stating how obedience is what matters to God, not an outward sign of circumcision, which on a non-believer is like a mark on a whitewashed tomb (Matthew 23:27; Acts 23:3). The sign of circumcision was first given to Abraham as an outward symbol of the covenant relationship he had with God (Genesis 17:10–11). It also served as a seal of the righteousness of his faith. The Law also demanded that every Jewish male be circumcised on the eighth day (Leviticus 12:3).

When Paul makes a statement concerning the identity of the true Jew, he is stating that there is something greater than being a blood descendant of Abraham, Isaac, and Jacob. God's Word tells how being a child of God is something other than a blood choice (Luke 3:8, Luke 16:24; John 8:33). Paul will soon discuss in a much deeper way how and why not all Israel is spiritual Israel (Romans 9:6) as Abraham has both a fleshy and a spiritual seed (Galatians 3:29).

God tells how the true believers have the circumcision that matters, one of the heart (Deuteronomy 10:16; Jeremiah 4:4). This circumcision is performed not by man but rather by the Holy Spirit (Colossians 2:11). This circumcision of the heart is what enables a believer to be a new creation and worship God in spirit (cf. Philippians 3:3; Galatians 6:15). The prophet Jeremiah told of a future day when God would punish those who were only circumcised in the flesh (uncircumcised in heart) (Jeremiah 9:25).

Make no mistake about this fact; Paul is defining true believers as having the circumcision of the heart. In this chapter, Paul has dealt with potential obstacles to the gospel. These included self-righteousness, the inadequacy of the Law, and the worthlessness of a fleshy circumcision. Paul also makes a very important argument, repeated throughout his Epistles.

The work of the Spirit is what matters because the the Law kills (2 Corinthians 3:6), while the Spirit gives life. This is a huge part of the gospel of Jesus Christ, which warns that those trying to obey the Law as a way to eternal life must do it perfectly. Since no one can profess perfection, this plan only leads to eternal death. The realization of this truth is what leads one to Jesus Christ.

CHAPTER THREE

The depravity of man, justification, redemption, and propitiation.

Verses 1–8

Paul now answers four typical Jewish response questions.

1) Read Romans 3:1–2

a) Verse 1: What two questions are asked?

b) Verse 2: Do the Jews have an advantage?

c) Verse 2: What were they entrusted with?

After telling how both Jews and Gentiles are equally guilty before God (Romans 2:11), Paul now deals with any doubt a Jew might have regarding their need for a Savior. He states that even though both the Gentiles and Jews are guilty before God, the Jews do have a great advantage (Romans 9:4).

Question 1: What advantage does the Jew have? Moses told of the blessed advantages of Israel (Deuteronomy 4:7–8). The Israelites were initially adopted as sons of God (Exodus 4:22; Romans 9:4). They could call on the Lord, and He would answer. They had His righteous Law to guide them. The Holy Spirit led the people while they were in the wilderness (Isaiah 63:11). The glory of the Lord was visible to all the people on Sinai (Exodus 24:16), in the tabernacle (Exodus 40:34), and the Temple (2 Chronicles 7:1). There were times God Himself also fought their battles (Exodus 14:25; Deuteronomy 20:4; Joshua 23:3; 2 Chronicles 20:29).

What about circumcision? Didn't Paul state that a circumcision of the heart was needed (Romans 2:29)? The answer is that circumcision was an outward sign that would serve to remind them of their covenant relationship with the God of all creation and the advantages that came with it. Unlike the Jews, the uncircumcised Gentiles (Ephesians 2:12–13) were strangers to God's covenant of promise and had no hope as they were without God in the world (Galatians 3:14; Genesis 22:18). Most importantly, the Jews were blessed and entrusted with the oracles of God (Acts 7:38). The prophets were Jews. Know that the Word of God is more important than any sacrifices, the ark, the priesthood, or the Sabbath.

While their blessings are things no other nation could claim, nothing compares with having been entrusted with the Word of God! Here are a few examples of how the God of the Bible protected His Word:

- God wrote the Commandments with his finger (Exodus 31:18).

- Moses wrote down all the words of the Lord (Exodus 24:4).

- The Law was stored by the Ark of the Covenant (Deuteronomy 31:24-26); later in the temple (2 Kings 22:8).

- Joshua added his words to the book of the Lord and put them in the treasury (Joshua 24:26).

- Samuel did the same (1 Samuel 10:25).

- Ezekiel wrote that there was an official register of prophets and their writings in the temple (Ezekiel 13:9).

- God told Moses (Deuteronomy 27:8), Isaiah (Isaiah 8:1, 30:8), Habakkuk (Habakkuk 2:2), and Jeremiah (Jeremiah 30:2, 36:2) to write His Words down.

2) Read Romans 3:3–4

a) Verse 3: What is the third question?

b) Verse 4: What is the answer?

c) Verse 4: What Old Testament Scripture did Paul quote?

In Chapter One, Paul told how the Old Testament reveals facts concerning the coming Messiah. The Old Testament revealed the faithfulness of God to His Word as He brought forth the Messiah despite the unfaithfulness of the Jewish people. Paul now makes it clear that God will not respond to the unfaithfulness of the Jews by forsaking His promises. Psalm 78 tells of God's faithfulness despite the Jews turning from Him. Notice how Paul talks about disbelief, the foundation of most other sins, which also prevents one from receiving the promises of God.

Notice how we are told God would be proven true even if every man is found to be a liar. Contrast this truth with the fact that the God of the Bible cannot lie (Titus 1:2). This should make it clear how those trusting in man are cursed (Jeremiah 17:5). Despite this fact, the masses trust and follow the wisdom of man instead of simply trusting in the faithful promises of God.

Question 2: Does that mean God will be unfaithful to His promises when people are unfaithful? Paul confirms how God will remain faithful to His promises by using the example of Psalm 51. This Psalm is important because it was written after Nathan had confronted David concerning his sin with Bathsheba (2 Samuel 12). In it, David is testifying to the faithfulness of God despite his own unfaithfulness. One of the marks of repentance is realizing God is true at the cost of the lies we've been telling ourselves. In a day when the truth is assumed to be determined by how many people believe it, God remains true even if everyone else believes something different!

3) Read Romans 3:5–6

a) Verse 5: What does man's unrighteousness reveal?

b) Verse 5: What is Paul's two-part question

c) Verse 6: What is the answer?

We are told that man's unrighteousness reveals God's righteousness and holiness. One could never fully appreciate how God is perfect and sinless without first seeing imperfection and sin. This awareness was accomplished through the Law given to the Jews, which exposed human sinfulness and clarified God's perfect standard. Paul deals with Jews who might have argued that their unrighteousness glorifies God.

Question 3: If their unrighteousness brings glory to God, would He not show them mercy in judgment, or can He rightfully judge them at all, since their sin has ultimately served to glorify Him? Paul responded that since God's judgment is impartial, righteous, and just, He will not show them any favoritism (Galatians 2:6). Paul also states that God could not judge the world if He were not just. This judgment will happen at the final judgment, which will happen after the millennium (Revelation 20:11–12).

4) Read Romans 3:7–8

a) Verse 7: What does the sin of lying do?

b) Verse 7: What is Paul's fourth question?

c) Verse 8: What doctrine was Paul accused of teaching?

d) Verse 8: What is Paul's response?

Question 4: How could the sin of lying be punished if it glorifies God? Isn't it amazing that man will go to ridiculous lengths to justify sinning? In this case, the Apostle Paul was accused of teaching the absurd doctrine that one should continue sinning as it ultimately glorifies God, a point he will return to in Chapter Six. Those who adhere to this doctrine are not Christians and are told that their condemnation is just. If true, this doctrine would bring dishonor to the name of God.

Realize that all sins result in judgment. While some might feel that they will not be judged for their sins, know that God will never overlook sin. Unlike what is taught in many churches, this is a major part of the gospel (Romans 1:18). With that being said, even today, many misunderstand the doctrine of grace, convinced it encourages sin. They disagree with the gospel of Jesus Christ, which they wrongly call "cheap grace," believing that, despite what Jesus did on the cross, they must somehow add to His work with things like good works, sacrifices, and attending church. Even though God loves us so much that He died for everyone (John 3:16; 2 Corinthians 5:15), they believe He is not the God of love He promises Himself to be (Matthew 25:24; 1 John 4:8).

Verses 9–20

Paul now confirms what he has just argued.
"The total depravity of man" both Jew and Gentile alike.

5) Read Romans 3:9–18

a) Verse 9: Are the Jews more righteous than Gentiles?

b) Verse 9: What do we know about both Jews and Gentiles?

c) Verse 10: Is anyone righteous?

d) Verses 11-18: List all the things we are told about mankind.

Making his case about the depravity of man, Paul confirms and summarizes his statement with the question, "What then?" He then makes fourteen points, quoting Psalms 14:1–3; 53:1–3; 5:9; 140:3; 10:7; Isaiah 59:7; and finally, Psalm 36:1 to show the powerful effects that sin has had on mankind, both Jew and Gentile. We are also shown how sin has affected mankind's minds, attitudes, words, and actions.

Sin has permeated man's entire being. Let's highlight the applications that Paul is making from Scripture:

- Sin has impacted man's ability to understand God.

- Sin has also affected mankind's emotions, causing him to turn from the one true God to idols.

- The result has been that no one seeks the true God, becoming useless in His eyes.

- Sin has affected mankind's actions, as this hardened state resulted in no one doing good.

- Man sins greatly with not only his mouth but his entire body.

- The results have been war, destruction, and misery for mankind throughout history.

- There is no hope for lasting peace.

- Man's soul and body experience total depravity.

- All due to not fearing the one true God.

Paul's argument clearly shows how depraved man has become. All due to sin! It also shows the hopelessness man finds himself in without Jesus. Without the conviction of the Holy Spirit, there would be no one who would seek after God (John 16:8). It is interesting how Paul sums up his points by stating that the people have no fear of God. Not fearing God is the root of all the sins that Paul has mentioned (Psalm 36:1; Proverbs 9:10). Paul now addresses any Jews who still consider themselves righteous due to the fact that they were under God's Law, assuming Paul had been speaking of the Gentiles and their depravity.

6) Read Romans 3:19–20

a) Verse 19: Exactly to whom does the Law speak?

b) Verse 19: What does the Law close?

c) Verse 19: What does the Law reveal to the whole world?

d) Verse 20: Can the Law justify anyone?

e) Verse 20: So why was the Law given?

Paul makes it clear that the previous verses also apply to the Jews who are under God's Law. He earlier told how the Gentiles have the work of the Law written on their heart (Romans 2:15), thus everyone is born into this world under the Law. The result is a keen awareness of one's unrighteousness. Few understand that the Law cannot establish righteousness, as it only condemns by revealing one's unrighteousness. How? By revealing exactly what sin is in God's sight.

God has mercifully given the Law to ensure that anyone under it is not only without excuse but also without a defense. This includes Jews and Gentiles. Paul tells how all this has been accomplished by revealing both sin and its destructive nature. This is so different from what religion teaches. It was also radically different from what the Jews had been taught. The result is that anyone under the Law has no righteousness (Psalm 143:2). The Law cannot save anyone. Because everyone is found to be a sinner, it closes every mouth (Romans 11:32).

Jesus alluded to this truth by telling the people they did not obey the Law (John 7:19). They responded by accusing Him of having a demon. While the Jews accepted the Law, they did not fully obey it and did not understand that complete obedience (perfection) was needed. Even today, many church-going people are not told that the Law has no provisions for eternal life (Galatians 3:21). Hearing this truth turned the Jews against both Stephen (Acts 6:13) and Paul (Acts 21:28). This realization about the Law is necessary if one is to appreciate and understand the doctrine of grace that Paul is now about to discuss.

Verses 21–26

Paul now gives the good news. One does not work for the righteousness needed for salvation!

7) Read Romans 3:21–24

a) Verse 21: What has been revealed apart from the Law?

b) Verse 21: Where and how was it foretold?

c) Verse 22: What is available through faith in Jesus?

d) Verse 22: How do we know it is available to both Jews and Gentiles?

e) Verse 23: Why is the righteousness of God needed?

f) Verse 24: How is this righteousness described?

g) Verse 24: How is this justification obtained?

Paul had just made a compelling argument that the Law cannot justify. He uses "but now" to transition into the good news that one can be saved apart from the Law. The gospel teaches that the righteousness of God is available by faith. Paul also tells how this was revealed by both the Law and the prophets, confirming what he had earlier stated (Romans 1:2). This truth shows how one can be saved without being under God's Law.

ROMANS 3:24 IS ONE OF THE MOST IMPORTANT VERSES IN THE ENTIRE BIBLE!

The righteousness of God is available by faith to everyone. Notice how it is also described as a gift. How do you reiceve a gift? By works? No, not by works. God's righteousness is revealed and available as a gift (without the Law) to everyone who puts their faith in the finished work of Jesus.

Why is it necessary to offer God's righteousness to everyone? Because all not only fall short of the glory of God, they do so in every way! Our helplessness because of sin makes our redemption by God necessary. God is righteous because He is faithful to the gospel, which says that God's righteousness is needed for salvation, and if you choose to put your faith in Christ, you are cleansed and saved (Romans 1:16–17). We will soon discuss exactly how and when this happens.

Take a moment and ask yourself these questions:

- *Do I understand that God's righteousness is what I need for salvation?*

- *Isn't God clear that this is a gift only available by faith?*

- *How is this different from what I have been taught?*

In Chapter One, Paul discussed how the Old Testament revealed facts about the coming Messiah, but what did it reveal about the righteousness of God? The fact that the Messiah would clothe believers with the robe of righteousness needed for salvation was witnessed by the prophets of the Old Testament (Isaiah 61:10; Jeremiah 23:6; Isaiah 45:8), and the life of Abraham (Romans 4:1–3). This is important because man cannot be righteous on his own, as all have sinned and fall short of the needed perfection. Those who now have this righteousness received it as a gift from God through Jesus Christ, who lived a perfect, obedient life, thereby earning the righteousness of those who put their faith in Him (1 Corinthians 1:30).

Look at Romans 3:24 again and notice the word *'justified.'* Now, notice how it is available as a gift. Justification is the answer to mankind's sin problem. This important word comes from the Greek *dikaioo*, which typically means *'declared righteous.'*

God is talking about one being declared righteous. Who does the declaring? God does! God declares everyone clothed with the righteousness of Jesus as righteous. This includes forgiveness and a declaration by the God of all creation that the justified individual is righteous before Him. One key part of the gospel is that justification is accomplished and based on the redemption which is in Christ Jesus (1 Corinthians 6:20).

While justification solves the righteousness problem, redemption solves the slavery to sin problem that Paul will soon discuss. The Greek word for *'redemption'* is *apolutrosis,* which means *'a release by payment of a ransom.'* Jesus satisfied the Father and delivered Christians by paying with His death the ransom required for their sins (1 Timothy 2:6; Matthew 20:28) and giving them His righteousness (Galatians 1:4; 1 Peter 1:18–19).

Catholics who die believing that their redemption was carried out by the sacrifice of the mass (Catechism 1364) will be disappointed to find out that contrary to what they were taught, Jesus died once and for all, and those who choose not to trust in this truth will die in their sins (Hebrews 10:10-11). This mission was accomplished when Jesus said with His dying breath, "It is finished" (John 19:30). We are told how, after ascending to Heaven, Jesus sat down (Hebrews 10:12–14), clearly showing that His work was finished.

8) Read Romans 3:25-26

a) Verse 25: How was Jesus publicly displayed?

b) Verse 25: How is His sacrifice described?

c) Verse 25: How are the benefits of His sacrifice obtained?

d) Verse 25: What was demonstrated?

e) Verses 25 & 26: How was God's righteousness demonstrated?

Jesus completely satisfied (propitiation) God's demands for sin with His shed blood. The Old Testament reveals how part of the Messiah's mission was to be an atoning sacrifice (Isaiah 53), which satisfied the wrath of God and removes the sins of those who put their faith in His finished work. This included shedding His blood (1 John 1:7), which cleanses believers of all (not just some) of their sins. Notice the importance of putting faith in the blood of Jesus—He exchanged His own life for yours. Leviticus 17:11, 14 tells us that *'blood'* and *'life'* are synonymous.

Ask yourself:

- *Do I believe that the blood of Jesus cleanses me from all sin?*

- *Do I understand that Jesus laying down His life for me was enough, or do I believe that other actions are needed?*

The fact that Jesus was publicly crucified on Calvary is an indisputable fact that even those of other religions acknowledge. Unlike what religion teaches, God has done for man what man could never do, that is, appease His wrath (Matthew 19:26).

Realize there is a difference between what one believes and what one chooses to put their faith and trust in. Many believe in Jesus. That is, He existed, died, and was raised from the dead. The gospel tells how the benefits of what Jesus did (eternal life) come to those who choose to place their faith in His work on their behalf. Until you *own* what Jesus did for you, He doesn't *own* you, even though you may believe certain things about Him. Jesus demonstrated God's righteousness by living a perfect, sin-free life (Hebrews 4:15).

Why was God was shown to be righteous as He had passed over the sins committed before Jesus' time? Because He knew of the coming sacrifice of His Son, which would be the only sacrifice needed for all time.

What about the Levitical sacrifices? They only covered sin (Hebrews 10:1–4) and were used to remind the people of their sinfulness.

Without the atoning sacrifice of Jesus, one might question: How could God be just if He passed over sin before the time of Jesus? Think of the Old Testament saints as being in a checkout line at the store (Hebrews 9:15). When they got to the cash register, they were allowed to pass by. Why? Because Jesus was at the back of the line, paying everyone's bill. In this case, it was death for their sins. And the same thing applies to us, born long after Jesus, who paid for our sins before we even sinned!

Why is this important? Because the Catholic Church wrongly teaches "that one must be purified from sin in a place called Purgatory (Catechism 1472)." Also taught is that "Purgatory is a place of fire that is necessary to atone for sin and cleanse the soul (Catechism 1031)."

Ask yourself how the same God who withheld judgment on those who lived before the time of Jesus, knowing He would pay the price for all sin, could now hold Christians eternally accountable for their sins. The answer is, He does not! Insisting we must atone even in part for our sins is disbelief and makes the sacrifice of Jesus on the cross ineffective.

To summarize this important Scripture: The righteousness of God was revealed not only by how He dealt with sin but also by how His righteousness is now available to those who put their trust in Him. God is and must be just in order to declare anyone else righteous!

Verses 27–31

Paul now argues against those who still believe justification has anything to do with works.

9) Read Romans 3:27–31

a) Verse 27: Is anyone able to boast?

b) Verse 27: How is salvation only available?

c) Verse 28: How is one justified?

d) Verse 29: What is God's relationship to both those under the Law (Jews) and those not (Gentiles)?

e) Verse 30: Does God justify both Jew (circumcised) and Greek (uncircumcised) by faith?

f) Verse 31: Does this truth nullify the Law?

Salvation is a gift! God is clear that no one in Heaven will be able to boast that they did anything to get there (Ephesians 2:8–9; 1 Corinthians 1:29). Notice how this is called the "law of faith." Jesus came to this earth to save sinners from their sins (1 Timothy 1:15). While the Word of God is clear, few trust in the gospel that tells how salvation is only available by faith (John 3:16). This realization is one reason there will one day be weeping and gnashing of teeth from those sent to hell (Matthew 25:30; Luke 13:28).

God does not have one standard for a Jew and another for a Gentile. Both groups are sinners needing a Savior (Romans 3:25). Paul reiterates how the Law does not establish righteousness. Since Jesus fulfilled the Law (Matthew 5:17), His righteousness is available to all, but only by faith. This truth does not nullify the Law, which was given to reveal what sin was and point people to Christ so they could be justified by faith (Galatians 3:24).

❖ ❖ ❖

This chapter focuses on the fact that God's righteousness is available to all and that the Old Testament tells of the coming gospel of righteousness by faith alone.

Take a moment to reflect on these truths, and answer these questions:

- *Do I recognize that I have no righteousness on my own?*

- *Have I been clothed with the righteousness of Jesus?*

- *Is my faith in Jesus alone?*

Know that His righteousness is only available by faith in His finished work.

CHAPTER FOUR

Abraham and David demonstrate righteousness by faith.

Before we discuss Chapter Four, let's review some highlights of the life of Abraham and the promises God made to him.

Genesis 12:1–3: God appeared and instructed an Aramean named Abram to leave Mesopotamia and, after settling in Haran (Genesis 15:7; Acts 7:2–3), to begin a journey to an unknown land where he would become the father of a people who would live in a place where they would be able to worship the one true God. The 75-year-old Abraham was also told that in him, all the families of the earth would be blessed. God did not, however, tell him how this would be done. Abram must have wondered how this could be since he and his wife, Sarai, were childless and advanced in age.

Genesis 12:7: After Abram, Sarai, and his nephew Lot arrived in Canaan, God promised He would bless Abram's descendants by giving them that specific land for their own possession. This land would later become known as the Promised Land.

Genesis 15:1–5: It was a few years later after Abram defeated four Babylonian kings who, while raiding the territory, had taken his nephew Lot prisoner. With Abram probably fearing retaliation, God promised His protection and that the elderly Abram would have a son. He then told Abram to look toward the heavens and count the stars, telling him that his descendants would be as numerous as the stars.

Genesis 15:6: Abram trusted in God's promise, and his faith alone was reckoned to him as righteousness.

Genesis 15:13: God established a covenant with Abram concerning the Promised Land and told him that his descendants would one day be oppressed in a strange land for four hundred years.

Genesis 15:18: God again reaffirmed His promise to Abram and even gave specific borders for the land He would give to the future nation of Israel. You can imagine the excitement of both Abram and Sarai concerning the Lord's promise of a son. You can also imagine their disappointment when, after many years, she still had not become pregnant.

Genesis 16:15: Not completely understanding God, an elderly Sarai told Abram to take their Egyptian slave Hagar as a wife. Eighty-six-year-old Abram was now blessed with a son named Ishmael, who would become the father of many Arab countries.

Genesis 17:5–8: Thirteen years later, the Lord again appeared and reaffirmed His covenant with Abram, which promised that he would be exceedingly fruitful and the father of many nations. He also changed his name to *Abraham,* which means *'father of a multitude.'* The covenant with the now ninety-nine-year-old Abraham and his future descendants was not only to give them the Promised Land but also to be their God. Thus, these specific children would belong to God, who promised He would give the Promised Land as an everlasting possession.

Genesis 17:10–12: The Lord then told Abraham the specifics of the covenant of circumcision, which would serve as a seal symbolizing the righteousness of Abraham's faith he had while still uncircumcised.

Genesis 17:15–16: God now promised that it would be ninety-year-old Sarai who would bear the promised son to Abraham. He also changed her name to *Sarah,* which meant *'princess.'*

Genesis 17:18–21: God confirmed that even though circumcised, His covenant was not through the illegitimate son Ishmael but through Abraham's promised son, who would be named Isaac. God also told Abraham that Isaac would be born within a year.

Genesis 17:24–26: Both the ninety-nine-year-old Abraham and Ishmael were circumcised.

Genesis 21:1–3: As promised, one-hundred-year-old Abraham and Sarah were blessed with a son they obediently named Isaac.

Genesis 22:17–18: After testing Abraham's faith with his son Isaac, God revealed more of His plan, telling Abraham how all the nations would one day be blessed by his seed. God's promises were only to Abraham and his seed (the coming Messiah), through whom all the nations would be blessed.

Verses 1–5

Justification by faith was evidenced in the life of Abraham.

1) Read Romans 4:1–2

a) Verses 1 & 2: What did Abraham find out?

b) Verse 2: Was Abraham justified by works before God?

c) Verse 2: Will Abraham boast in heaven?

By talking about our forefather according to the flesh, Paul seems to be directing this to Jewish readers of this letter who identified with Abraham and might have argued that it was his works that set him apart (Matthew 3:9; John 8:37). You have to keep in mind that the typical Jewish mindset was all about the Law and the works of obedience it demanded. To hear that faith alone is counted as righteousness would have been perceived as contradicting what they had been taught. Paul now points out how the Old Testament reveals that God justified people by faith. Even today, this good news is opposite to what the present church in Rome teaches, that justification is through works that are necessary for salvation (Catechism 1815–16).

Now, if anyone could boast about his works, it might be Abraham. He left his home and settled in Haran (Genesis 12:4), about six hundred miles from Ur, where God first called him. This great patriarch obeyed God by leaving his family to begin a journey, not knowing where he was going. He also obeyed God to the point of being prepared to offer up his son, Isaac. Yet we are told that Abraham could not boast before God. Why? Paul is about to tell us.

2) Read Romans 4:3–5

a) Verse 3: What does Scripture say was reckoned to Abraham as righteousness?

b) Verse 4: Can salvation be called a gift if work is necessary to obtain it?

c) Verse 5: Is faith being credited as righteousness available to everyone?

d) Verse 5: Does God also justify the ungodly?

e) Verse 5: What is credited as righteousness?

Paul points out that despite all of Abraham's works, Scripture says he could not boast because he was justified by faith, not his obedience. Paul confirms what he had just stated (Romans 3:27). Faith alone is what is important. God tells those who pursue righteousness to look to Abraham as an example of how to obtain it (Isaiah 51:1–2).

What do we find that Scripture plainly states about Abraham's righteousness? Abraham (the father of the Jewish people) believed God's promise and was justified by faith (Genesis 15:6); thus, he had no grounds to boast before God. Because works cannot justify, there will be no one in Heaven who will be able to boast before God (Ephesians 2:8–9).

Know that Romans (Romans 4:2–3) clearly shows how the Epistle of James (James 2:24) tells how works cannot justify one before God, as they only reveal one's righteousness before man. This contradicts anyone using James to prove that works somehow justify either Abraham or man. Works and obedience are a byproduct and confirmation of authentic faith (Ephesians 2:8–10), not a substitute for faith.

Again, Abraham's faith was counted as righteousness (Galatians 3:6). Let me repeat that faith and not works result in being credited with the righteousness of Jesus. This is good news to one who realizes their work cannot save them, and contrary to religion erroneously teaching that works somehow result in God "owing" man something (Romans 11:6).

Paul explains how work is rightly rewarded with pay, and faith in God is credited as righteousness. Paul now explains how this gift is available to all who exercise faith, just like Abraham did. The God of the Bible wants us to believe what He says. Without faith, it is impossible to please Him (Hebrews 11:6). How can we apply this important truth? By trusting in what God says! But can He be trusted? Is His Word hard to understand?

Ask yourself these personal application questions. Know that your answers will determine where you will spend eternity.

- *Do I believe that I can be credited with God's righteousness by faith alone?*

- *Do I want to trust God's righteousness or my own?*

- *Hasn't the God of the Bible made it clear that you can have no righteousness on your own?*

The righteousness one is credited with is the perfect righteousness of Jesus Christ! This was true even of Abraham, demonstrated by Jesus' claim, "Before Abraham was, I am" (John 8:58). This promise of faith being credited with righteousness is for everyone and even includes those considered ungodly. The real truth is that all were ungodly before becoming a Christian (Matthew 9:12–13; Mark 2:17). This is so important. All have sinned and fallen short of the glory of God (Romans 3:23). Realizing one's total depravity is necessary to seek justification by faith! While works are important in the life of a believer, they are not part of the gospel, clearly stating that a man is justified by faith alone!

Why is it important to know that justification is by faith alone? Because many so-called Christian religions have perverted the gospel by stressing works as if they were necessary for salvation. Works can and do reveal one's faith to others, since only God knows the hearts of men (Proverbs 15:11; Acts 1:24) and people can easily deceive others (Matthew 7:21–22), but they are not necessary for salvation.

◆ ◆ ◆

Verses 6–8

David also spoke of the blessing of having his sins covered due to
his faith being reckoned as righteousness.

3) Read Romans 4:6–8

a) Verse 6: Who does David say is blessed?

b) Verses 7 & 8: What does this justification include?

Paul now deals with the possible argument that justification by faith ended with the giving of the Law or was lost by sin. He reminds us how King David wrote of the blessing of being reckoned righteous and justified without works. Notice how this blessing includes sins covered by the blood of Jesus (Psalm 32:1–2), resulting in complete forgiveness (Colossians 1:14).

Why is David's example important? David wrote Psalm 32:1–2 sometime after his sin with Bathsheba (2 Samuel 11), the murder of Uriah, and his efforts to conceal it. This shows that David believed justification was by faith and not lost due to sin.

Why are all Christians, whose sins God will not take into account (Romans 8:1; 2 Corinthians 5:19), considered blessed? Because justification includes forgiveness. Know that just as Paul stated (Romans 3:21), this gospel is witnessed by both Abraham and David.

The present-day church at Rome wrongly teaches that justification is lost through mortal sin (Catechism 1033, 1855, 1874) and only regained through the sacrament of confession (Catechism 1446), but the Word of God clearly teaches that justification happens at conversion and is never lost.

❖ ❖ ❖

Verses 9–12

Abraham's justification happened well before he was circumcised.

4) Read Romans 4:9–10

a) Verse 9: What question does Paul ask?

b) Verse 9: What was credited to Abraham as righteousness?

c) Verse 10: Did this take place before or after Abraham was circumcised?

Paul now deals with a possible Jewish response to the previous examples of Abraham and David, "Is this blessing of being righteous by faith for the Jew (circumcised) or the Gentile (uncircumcised)?" The answer is that God's blessing comes to all and is only available by faith (Romans 4:5).

When did this blessing of faith being reckoned as righteousness come to Abraham? While he was still uncircumcised. The Jews would have considered an uncircumcised Abraham a Gentile. God declared Abraham righteous (Genesis 15:6), and he was not circumcised until fourteen years later (Genesis 17:24–

26).

Why is the timing of Abraham's circumcision so important? It confirms how faith, not works of the Law, was credited as righteousness. If Abraham could be righteous without circumcision, then any Gentile can also be righteous without being circumcised (Galatians 5:2). This argument would be especially impactful to a Jew who thought circumcision was necessary to inherit any promises from God. God gave Abraham the covenant of circumcision, which ratified the covenant relationship the descendant Jewish male had with God (Genesis 17:11–12). The typical Jew viewed circumcision and the Law as what set them apart from the other nations.

Paul has already dealt with the Law (Romans 2) and now deals with circumcision. We are told in the letter to the Galatians how Judaizers had come and wrongly told the people that to be saved, they must be circumcised (in the flesh). Paul's response was circumcision is not any part of the gospel of Jesus Christ (Galatians 1:6). Works cannot justify (Galatians 2:16). Paul also stated that it was either circumcision or Christ (Galatians 5:2).

Why won't those who trusted in works (circumcision) not benefit from the finished work of Jesus? Because they were not placing their faith in Jesus alone.

5) Read Romans 4:11–12

a) Verse 11: What was Abraham's circumcision a seal of?

b) Verse 11: Did Abraham have this faith before he was circumcised?

c) Verses 11 & 12: What two types of people is Abraham a father to?

Paul now deals with the hypothetical question a Jew might have concerning circumcision, asking, "If circumcision isn't that important, then why did God tell Abraham to be circumcised?" It was fourteen years after being declared righteous (Genesis 17:24–6) that Abraham received the sign of circumcision, which was a seal or mark that bore witness to the righteousness he had (due to his faith) while he was still uncircumcised. It would also serve as a reminder of his covenant relationship with God. The result is that Abraham is the model of justification by faith that is now available to not only Jews (as they believed) but also Gentiles, making Abraham the symbolic father to all believers (both Jews and Gentiles) (Galatians 3:7).

Let me repeat that the circumcision of Abraham only served as a seal or mark that signified the righteousness of the faith he had while uncircumcised. Thus, his righteousness had nothing to do with either circumcision or the Law. The key point that Paul is making about Abraham is his faith, not his circumcision. Paul earlier told of the importance of a more important heart circumcision (Romans 2:28–29), performed by the Holy Spirit (Deuteronomy 30:6; Jeremiah 9:25). Know that this circumcision is also a seal or mark of the righteousness of a Christian (due to faith) without any works, let alone being circumcised in the flesh (Colossians 2:11; Ephesians 1:13, 4:30).

Verses 13–22

Paul now explains the importance of Abraham's faith.

6) Read Romans 4:13–14

a) Verse 13: What was God's promise to Abraham?

b) Verse 13: Was God's promise to Abraham available through the Law?

c) Verse 13: Exactly how was it available?

d) Verse 14: What happens if those under the Law are heirs?

Paul now deals with a possible Jewish response that Abraham was their father and not the father to the Gentiles (Matthew 3:9; Luke 3:8; John 8:39). They believed their lineage to Abraham entitled them to blessings not promised to Gentiles. But God had promised Abraham that through him all the nations would be blessed (Genesis 12:1–3).

How could God's promise to Abraham be tied to the Law when the timing was over four hundred and thirty years before God even gave it to Moses (Galatians 3:17)? God changed Abram's name to Abraham and promised that he would be the father of a multitude of nations (Genesis 17:5). All of this meant not only the Jewish nation but also Gentile nations would also have access to God's promises, clearly showing the blessing of Abraham is for everyone (Galatians 3:7).

God then got more specific with Abraham, telling him that in his seed, all the nations would be blessed (Genesis 22:18). Notice how God did not use the word "seeds" but rather "seed." This would be fulfilled and accomplished through Jesus Christ (Galatians 3:16), with the result being all Christians are now heirs to the promise God made to Abraham due to the fact they make up the body of Christ, who is the promised seed (Galatians 3:29). This includes both Jew and Gentile (Isaiah 63:16).

In his letter to the Galatians (Galatians 3:16–18), Paul argued that since a covenant made between men cannot be changed or broken, a covenant made by the never-changing God could never be broken (Malachi 3:6). This shows how the Law (which came over four hundred years after the time of Jacob) did not and cannot add to or nullify God's promises to Abraham and his seed.

The application of this truth is that God's covenant with Abraham has precedence over the Law. Paul is clear that the Law and faith are, in fact, in opposition to each other (Galatians 3:18). God's promise to Abraham was a blessing, not a curse. Remember, those under the Law are not heirs of salvation. They are, in fact, cursed (Galatians 3:10). If God's promise to Abraham was predicated on his obedience, it would have made it worthless. If obeying the Law is necessary for salvation, faith and God's promises are void. One needs to be able to trust God. Faith is the assurance of God's promises (Hebrews 11:1).

7) Read Romans 4:15–16

a) Verse 15: What does the Law bring?

b) Verse 15: Is there wrath for those not under the Law?

c) Verse 16: How is the promise available?

d) Verse 16: Why?

e) Verse 16: Exactly who is it available to?

f) Verse 16: How is Abraham referred to?

God's Law had no provisions for eternal life (Galatians 3:21), only earthly blessings for obedience and curses for disobedience. Know that those under the Law are cursed since no one can obey the Law; it only brings wrath (Galatians 3:9). Paul tells how those free from the Law are blessed, as there is no violation. But how can one become free from the Law? Paul will soon answer this most important question.

Paul summarizes his argument by again stressing that the promise of God is that justification is a guaranteed gift available to everyone by faith, both Jew and Gentile. Thus, Christians are saved by grace through faith (Ephesians 2:8–9). This truth was witnessed in the life of Abraham, who received the promises of God by faith. Those who receive Jesus (John 1:12) are heirs of God's promise to Abraham (Genesis 22:18), as they make up His body (Galatians 3:26–29). Thus, God's promise to Abraham is fulfilled as he is the father of those who have the same faith as his, both Jew and Gentile (Genesis 17:4–5). Notice how God states salvation is by faith, so His promise is guaranteed. Meditate on this truth.

If God's promise is by works, how could anyone ever know or be sure they would inherit it? This would naturally lead to doubting, which itself prevents one from receiving the gift He has given. It is such a blessing to trust what God promises.

8) Read Romans 4:17–22

a) Verse 17: What promise does Paul stress?

b) Verse 17: What did Abraham trust that God was able to do?

c) Verses 17 & 18: How did Abraham respond to God's promise?

d) Verse 19: What was the result?

e) Verse 19: What did Abraham realize about himself and Sarah?

f) Verse 20: What did Abraham choose to believe?

g) Verse 21: What did Abraham come to realize?

h) Verse 22: What was the result of Abraham's faith?

Paul now exhorts those who might doubt the promises of God, who told Abram to look up and count the stars, promising that his descendants would be as numerous (Genesis 15:5). Keep in mind that there was no light pollution in Abram's time. Think about how many stars he could normally see on a clear night. Imagine how many times Abraham looked up at the stars and then reminded himself of God's promise (Hebrews 11:12). God changed Abram's name to Abraham and told him that he would be the father of many nations (Genesis 17:5). Abraham chose to believe God (Genesis 17:17–21) even though he was ninety-nine years old and his wife Sarah was eighty-nine years old, considerably past childbearing years (Genesis 17:17, 18:11).

Abraham knew and trusted that nothing is too difficult for the God of the Bible (Genesis 18:14; Jeremiah 32:27). Many times people make the mistake of looking at their circumstances, instead of trusting in what the Word of God says. Despite the apparent discouraging reality facing Abraham, he chose to walk by faith and not by sight (2 Corinthians 5:7).

Take a moment and think about the life of Abraham. You can imagine how excited he was when, at the age of seventy-five, he was called out of Haran by God, who promised that He would give his descendants the land of Canaan (Genesis 12:1–7). Remember, at this time, Abraham was childless. I imagine him wondering, "Did I hear right? I will have descendants?" You can imagine that Abraham was very excited when, a few years later, he was told by the Lord that he would have a son (Genesis 15:4). You can also imagine Abraham being somewhat discouraged when, years later, he still didn't have a son. But Abraham grew strong in faith, being assured that God was able to bring about what He promised. Isn't that the key? Isn't this what Paul is preaching? God Himself promises justification by faith. Can we trust this truth, or do we trust men telling us something else?

Ask yourself:

- *Am I fully assured that God will perform exactly what He promised?*

- *What prevents me from placing my complete trust in Him?*

IF YOU HAVE NOT YET COMMITTED YOUR LIFE AND TRUST TO JESUS, DON'T WAIT ANOTHER MINUTE. DO IT NOW.

We are told how Abraham not only trusted God but also gave glory to Him while doing so. You can imagine Abraham looking at his circumstances and thanking God that they didn't matter, as He could do anything (Hebrews 11:6). Notice how Paul once again stresses justification by emphasizing that Abraham was justified by faith by simply trusting God. Abraham was convinced that the Almighty God of all creation was able to do what He promised!

Verses 23–25

Paul now tells how this example of Abraham applies to our lives.

9) Read Romans 4:23–25

a) Verse 23: Was the story of Abraham only applicable to him?

b) Verses 23 & 24: Why is Abraham's justification by faith so important to us?

c) Verses 24 & 25: What must one believe in order to be justified?

How can we apply what the Word of God teaches about Abraham? By trusting that God will credit our faith in Jesus Christ as the righteousness needed for eternal life! Just as Abraham knew that his body was as good as dead, yet believed that God would do as He promised, Christians believe that Jesus was crucified for their sins and then raised from the dead. Jesus died for all sins and was then raised so that those who place their faith in Him can have new life. Notice how Paul writes that these things are written so everyone who trusts in Jesus will know they have the same justification by faith that Abraham had.

The resurrection of Jesus demonstrated that the Father's wrath was completely satisfied with His sacrifice. Know that Christians would not have life without the resurrection of Jesus. The risen Christ not only proved the deity of Jesus (Romans 1:4) but also that the Father accepted His sacrifice. The resurrection of Jesus also bore witness to His righteousness.

The Word of God is very clear on the subject of justification by faith. Let us review the important points that Paul has made in this chapter:

- Justification is by faith and not works (Romans 4:1-6, 18-22).

- Justification is not lost by sin (Romans 4:7-8).

- Justification has no connection to a fleshy circumcision (Romans 4:9-11).

- Justification is not superseded by the Law (Romans 4:13-16).

- Justification by faith is available to all who trust in Jesus (Romans 4:23-25).

CHAPTER FIVE

The results and benefits of our justification.

Verses 1–5

The results and benefits of the justification that comes by faith in Jesus.

1) Read Romans 5:1–2

a) Verse 1: Exactly how is one justified?

b) Verse 1: What is one benefit of justification?

c) Verse 2: Through whom is justification available?

d) Verse 2: How is justification available?

e) Verse 2: In what do Christians now stand?

f) Verse 2: What can all Christians exult in?

Notice how Paul writes, "having been justified by faith," clearly showing how this only happens once. Using David as the example (Romans 4:7–8), Paul has also shown how this justification is not lost by sin. After previously making his point that justification is not based on works, Paul now uses the word "therefore," turning to the benefits that all believers now have.

THE FIRST BENEFIT OF JUSTIFICATION IS PEACE WITH GOD!

Contrast this with God earlier declaring how He has wrath toward sinners (Romans 1:18) and that there is a coming day of judgment (Romans 2:5). Remember, non-Christians are under God's Law which only brings about wrath (Romans 4:15). Christians will not experience God's wrath (1 Thessalonians 1:10, 5:9), but have been declared righteous, ensuring they have peace with Him (Ephesians 2:14: Colossians 1:20).

Can God be any clearer concerning justification? Christians are justified by faith and have peace with God (2 Corinthians 5:19-20). While many religions teach otherwise, the gospel is truly good news. Realize that it is the devil who opposes the truth of God and, through religion, has attempted to change the gospel from grace to works (John 8:44). Many people accept this heresy because they are ignorant of what God says about the most important subject matter in their lives. They don't realize God pronounces a curse on those who trust in man rather than Him (Jeremiah 17:5). This should come as no surprise as God warns that the devil will come disguised as an angel of light (2 Corinthians 11:14). Justification is a gift that comes only by faith and is only available through Jesus Christ (Ephesians 2:8-9). Paul tells how those justified (Christians) now stand by the grace of God (1 Corinthians 15:1).

THE SECOND BENEFIT OF JUSTIFICATION IS THAT THROUGH JESUS, CHRISTIANS CONTINUALLY STAND (OR LIVE) IN GRACE.

Believers now have grace through which they also have access to God—a privilege that no one except the Jewish High Priest previously had (Ephesians 2:18), and even then, only on the Day of Atonement (Leviticus 16:1–34). This access is not lost due to sin and enables believers to have an ongoing relationship with God. When Jesus died, the veil of the Temple was torn, symbolizing that everyone now has access to God (Matthew 27:51). The rending of the massive curtain showed that this access to Him is only through Jesus Christ (John 14:6; 1 Timothy 2:5). Paul tells how Christians can boast in the future glory they will soon experience when they meet Jesus face to face (1 Corinthians 13:12; Revelation 22:4). This blessing is received as a gift from God.

2) Read Romans 5:3–5

a) Verse 3: What else results from justification?

b) Verse 3: What do Christians do in their tribulations?

c) Verses 3 & 4: What do trials bring forth?

d) Verse 5: How has God poured out His love toward believers?

We are told how an additional fruit of justification is how a Christian will exult or rejoice in their tribulations (Luke 6:22; Acts 5:41; 1 Peter 4:14): How can this happen? Because Christians have peace with God and a sure hope for the future. They know that they have eternal life no matter what. The relationship that Christians have with God is what enables them to have this hope.

CHAPTER FIVE

A typical Jew, understanding that the Law promised blessings for obedience and curses for disobedience, might relate any trials to sin and ask, "How can you endure trials if your sin is already atoned for?" The followers of Jesus will have tribulation in this life (John 16:33). Remember, we live in a fallen world that endures the effects of the original sin of Adam. Some preach a false prosperity gospel that states God wants everyone to be rich and healthy. If true, Paul would not have described this benefit of peace in trials. While peace with God does not always equate to peace on earth, it will give a believer the proper eternal perspective needed to endure the trials we are guaranteed to face (John 15:20; 1 Thessalonians 3:3).

Why does God allow trials in believers? One answer is that trials distinguish the true believers from the impostors (Matthew 13:21), who will eventually fall away from the faith (1 John 2:19). Trials test one's faith in God. I have witnessed professed believers responding to a trial by blaming God and then falling away from Him. When Paul says to rejoice in our tribulations, it is because they test your faith in God (Psalm 119:116), ultimately bringing endurance, which results in spiritual maturity and greater character. Trials also reveal who we are in Christ, allowing us to have a sure hope in the Lord. The Epistle of James also tells how the testing of faith produces endurance (James 1:2–4). So, how you deal with a trial reveals your true identity.

THE THIRD BENEFIT OF JUSTIFICATION IS THAT THE HOLY SPIRIT IS GIVEN TO CHRISTIANS (1 CORINTHIANS 6:19; 2 CORINTHIANS 13:5).

What a blessing! Jesus told His disciples it was better that He leave so the Holy Spirit would come (John 16:7). This is the first mention of Him in this epistle. The Holy Spirit has been given as a down payment on our salvation, allowing us to have a sure hope (2 Corinthians 1:22, 5:5; Ephesians 1:13–14). The Holy Spirit is the one who gives us the strength to withstand the tribulations that are sure to come into our lives. The indwelling Holy Spirit distinguishes Christians from those in the world (Romans 8:8–10). Paul has told how those who are justified experience the love and peace of God, enabling them to exult (take joy) in their sure hope of eternal life.

Verses 6–8

The depth of God's love toward us!

3) Read Romans 5:6–8

a) Verse 6: How is everyone described?

b) Verse 6: What did Jesus do for everyone?

c) Verse 7: What two character traits are mentioned?

d) Verse 7: Were you either one of these before becoming a Christian?

e) Verse 8: How does God describe those not justified?

f) Verse 8: How did God demonstrate His love for us?

Without Jesus's victory (John 8:25–32), everyone is helpless against sin (Romans 4:5). Notice how Paul has described non-believers as helpless, ungodly, and sinners. All non-Christians are weak, helpless, and powerless to deliver themselves from the sin that has hold of them. Unlike what religion teaches, no one can do anything to make themselves righteous in God's eyes. Knowing this and loving us so much, God sent His only Son to die for us (John 3:16) even though we were neither righteous nor good in His eyes. God states that the soul who sins must die (Ezekiel 18:4), but Jesus died in our place. Realize that there was no other way of escape except the sacrificial death of Christ. This is a major part of the gospel.

Verses 9–11

The future benefits of justification.

4) Read Romans 5:9–11

a) Verse 9: How have Christians been justified?

b) Verse 9: What have Christians been saved from?

c) Verse 10: How are non-Christians described?

d) Verse 10: How are believers reconciled to God?

e) Verse 10: What is the benefit of this?

f) Verse 11: Who will Christians rejoice in for eternity?

Once again, Paul uses the term "we have now been justified," showing how justification is a one-time event in the life of a Christian. It is the death of Jesus and His shed blood that allows Christians to be in right standing with Him (Romans 3:25). God's Word is clear that Christians will be spared and not experience God's future wrath (1 Thessalonians 1:10, 5:9). Christians have been given life by the Holy Spirit who lives inside them (2 Corinthians 13:5).

Because non-Christians are concerned with the things of the world (James 4:4) and of the flesh (Galatians 5:19–21), they are by nature enemies of God (Ephesians 2:3). We were just told how non-Christians are helpless sinners in need of a Savior (Romans 5:6–8). This means all Christians at one time lived their lives acting as enemies of God. Despite this fact, Jesus gave His life for all sinners so that those who put their trust in Him could be reconciled to God and saved from His coming wrath toward all sin, which will not be fully demonstrated until the final judgment (Romans 1:18).

Paul tells how Christians were reconciled to God. This is due to the justification that happens only once and is not lost by sin. Because of this fact, Christians will only experience the judgment that will determine the reward for their deeds done on earth (Bema) (2 Corinthians 5:10). All non-believers will have to experience the Great White Throne judgment (Revelation 20:11–12). Christians have access to the Father that non-believers do not have (John 14:6; Ephesians 2:18; 1 Timothy 2:5).

So far in this chapter, Paul has told how those justified have:

- Peace with God

- Access to Him through the grace we now stand in

- Joy in our tribulations.

- The indwelling Holy Spirit.

- Freedom from the coming wrath of God due to the fact that we have been reconciled to Him.

Take a moment and dwell on those blessings Christians have received through God's grace! This clearly shows the differences between those who are not justified and Christians who have been clothed with Jesus Christ's righteousness. It also shows how justification impacts a Christian's present life and future.

◆ ◆ ◆

Verses 12–14

Original sin and its ramifications on mankind.

5) Read Romans 5:12–14

a) Verse 12: How did sin enter the world?

b) Verse 12: How did death come to be?

c) Verse 12: Why does everyone die?

d) Verse 13: Was sin present in the world before God gave the Law to Moses?

e) Verse 13: What happens to sin without the Law?

f) Verse 14: Was death present before God gave the Law?

g) Verse 14: What does this show concerning mankind's state before God?

h) Verse 14: How is Adam described?

Paul explains why Christ's actions were necessary, showing how justification by faith overcomes the effects of Adam's original sin. Through Adam, all his descendants inherited not only a sinful nature but also guilt before a perfect God. Since that time, everyone born is considered "in Adam," who is the symbolic head of the human race. Those "in Adam" are enemies of God, guilty and helpless in their battle with sin. Since sin is passed on through man, Jesus could not be born into Adam's lineage (1 Corinthians 15:21–22) and had to be born of a virgin (Isaiah 7:14; Matthew 1:21–25). Without an earthly father, Jesus had neither inherited guilt nor acquired sin (1 Peter 1:19). We should now better understand why He is called the "last Adam" (1 Corinthians 15:45).

While I was taught that I was born with the stain of original sin, a better description would be original guilt. In fact, I was guilty before I was even born. This truth is why Job told how no one born of a woman could be pure or righteous (Job 15:14), and David stated that he was brought forth in iniquity (Psalm 51:5). Death is not only a result of sin (Genesis 2:17) but also a symptom of the guilt inherited from Adam. Because all are guilty in Adam, death reigned in mankind even before God gave Moses the Law (Romans 2:12). This includes many who would not have been considered guilty of committing major sins. This clearly shows how everyone "in Adam" is guilty before a holy God. This guilt is with or without the Law, which we now know was given to define sin (Romans 3:20) and to show mercy to all (Romans 11:32).

Just as sin came and caused death through one man, it is through one man (Jesus) that the opportunity for life can now come to everyone. When Paul talks about Adam being a type of Him who was to come, he sets the stage to describe different people who are separate from those described as "in Adam." While everyone born into this world has been impacted by the "one man" Adam's sin, everyone also has a chance to be impacted by the life and death of the "one man" Jesus Christ. Realize that anyone desiring reconciliation with God must be moved from being "in Adam" to another group with Jesus Christ as the head (2 Corinthians 5:19), with these people considered "in Christ."

❖ ❖ ❖

Verses 15–22

The differences between Adam's sin and Christ's gift of salvation.

6) Read Romans 5:15–19

    a) Verses 15 & 16: How is salvation described?

    b) Verses 15 &16: What happened as a result of Adam's sin?

    c) Verse 15: Who is God's gift available from?

    d) Verses 15 & 18: Who is God's gift available to?

    e) Verse 17: What is the free gift?

    f) Verses 16 & 18: What does the gift result in?

    g) Verse 17: What will those who receive God's gift reign in?

    h) Verse 19: How are the works of Adam and Jesus contrasted?

Paul now shows the contrast between the original sin of Adam and Jesus Christ, whose obedience was even to the point of death (Philippians 2:8). While Adam's single sin brought guilt (Genesis 2:16–17), resulting in the penalty of death to all of mankind (1 Corinthians 15:21), Jesus and His perfect obedience brought justification, nullified death, and brought eternal life to all believers (1 Corinthians 15:21; 2 Timothy 1:10). God's grace abounds through the free gift (available only through Jesus), which not only removed the effects of the original sin but also resulted in the perfect righteousness that is necessary for salvation, now being available to everyone (1 Corinthians 1:30). This is something Adam did not have before the fall.

Be clear about this point: God's gift of righteousness results in justification for the one receiving it. This is how God can declare all Christians as righteous. This gift is not of works and is only available by faith (Ephesians 2:8–9). Only those who receive Christ's righteousness will reign in eternal life. Recognize that Jesus lived a perfectly obedient life (Hebrews 4:15), therefore earning the righteousness needed to qualify Christians for eternal life (Colossians 1:12).

This truth is so important that it must not only be understood but also able to be shared with others. God has determined that perfection is the standard for eternal life (Matthew 5:48), something impossible for man to achieve (Matthew 19:25–26). Knowing this, Jesus came to this earth and lived a perfect, sin-free life (2 Corinthians 5:21), thus becoming the only source of the righteousness needed for eternal life (1 Corinthians 1:30; Hebrews 5:9).

The biblical term *'justification'* means *'declared righteous.'* When someone places their faith in Jesus, they are clothed with His righteousness (Isaiah 61:10). This is how the Father can look at the spirit of a Christian and declare them righteous. This justification is not by works (Romans 4:5–6) and not lost by sin (Romans 4:7–8; 2 Corinthians 5:19). This is how a Christian can state that Jesus is their righteousness (Isaiah 45:24; Jeremiah 23:5; Philippians 3:9). What a blessing it is to know that salvation is in Christ Jesus alone!

7) Read Romans 5:20–21

a) Verse 20: What was the result of the Law?

b) Verse 20: How did God respond to increased sin?

c) Verse 21: What does sin reign in?

d) Verse 21: What does grace use to reign in?

After describing how man was guilty before the giving of God's Law (Romans 5:13–14), Paul now informs us that the Law increased transgression. God knew before He gave the Law how it would increase sin (Romans 3:20; Galatians 3:19) by revealing and confronting it. He also knew that anyone under the Law would be shown to be a slave to sin (Romans 6:14; 1 Corinthians 15:56). Paul will expound on this subject in the next chapter.

Why did God give the Law if He knew it would increase sin? He did so knowing that He was showing mercy by revealing to everyone that they were sinners in need of a Savior (Galatians 3:22; Romans 11:32). Remember, it was the sin of Adam and not the Law that made everyone sinners. The Law simply removed any excuse; we're all sinners before God's standard. Under the Law, the effects of Adam's original sin became even more pronounced and visible. This also reveals God's grace, which includes the righteousness of Jesus Christ. This, too, was part of God's eternal plan!

Paul closes the chapter by contrasting sin and the death it brings with God's gift of righteousness (through Jesus Christ) and the eternal life it brings. God's grace, which included both the death and resurrection of Jesus Christ, has completely reversed and removed the effects of the original sin.

Reflect on this chapter and look at the four times Paul uses the phrase "much more" to show the superiority of what Jesus has done (Romans 5:9, 10, 15, 17). Even though sin has destructive consequences, God's grace allows us to do much more than simply overcome them. He has saved us from His wrath by declaring us righteous, and has not only reconciled us but also given us eternal life.

CHAPTER SIX

Christians have freedom from sin's power.

Verses 1–14

Paul talks about the freedom from sin's power that Christians now have.

1) Read Romans 6:1–4

    a) Verse 1: What question is asked?

    b) Verse 2: What is the answer?

    c) Verse 2: Why not?

    d) Verses 3 & 4: What has happened to Christians?

    e) Verse 4: What is the result?

Romans Chapter Five talked of both the present and future benefits of our justification. Paul now talks about another important benefit of justification, which involves freedom from sin's power and enables Christians to live obedient lives. Realize that this freedom directly impacts the sanctification of a Christian. Paul stated in the last chapter that God responded to increased sin and awareness of sin (due to the Law) with more grace (Romans 5:20–21). But he knew his readers would be tempted to use grace as a license to sin. So, he now answers the hypothetical response by explaining how and why Christians are different.

Read verse one again. Note that if salvation were a result of works, this question would not be asked, thus proving that salvation is not by works or obedience. As ridiculous as it seems, the doctrine and sin of licentiousness were something the early church had to deal with, as people were taught that their continued sinning was covered by God's grace (Jude 1:4; Galatians 5:13). Misunderstanding and practicing this false application would give people the false assurance that they were free to indulge in the desires of the flesh, concluding that God would simply shed more grace to cover their sins.

Paul, who himself was accused of this heresy (Romans 3:8), now deals with it by stating "may it never be," pointing out how, through baptism into Christ's death, Christians have died to sin. Therefore, Christians are not only expected to obey God, but they are also empowered to do so. Many argue against the concept of grace, believing that it equates to a freedom to sin. They fail to understand that Christians are free from sin's power and are motivated to obey God (Ezekiel 36:26–27). You can't be a Christian and live in sin (1 John 3:9).

How can you live in something that you have died to? The answer is you can't.

Does this mean that Christians don't sin? No, but they have a different relationship with sin than they once had, something Paul will soon expound on.

This truth illustrates the superiority of the New Covenant over the Law. Christians died to sin when they placed their faith in Jesus and were justified (Galatians 2:19–20). This is due to the fact that they were baptized into Christ's death and His resurrection (Colossians 3:1). Without the death of Jesus, no one could be buried with Him in baptism. This shows that Christ had to die. I was once shocked when told by a Catholic religious education director that it was important for Jesus to come to this earth, but He didn't really have to die. Know that this heresy has now permeated not only the Catholic religion but many other so-called Christian religions.

Do you think that God Himself would come to this earth and allow Himself to be crucified if it wasn't necessary? Jesus Himself taught that He must suffer, be killed, and then be raised (Matthew 16:21; Luke 24:26). While God states that the soul who sins must die (Ezekiel 18:4), Jesus paid the price of death for everyone (Hebrews 2:9). Let me also point out that the death of Messiah was necessary to institute the New Covenant (Hebrews 9:15–17). Without His death, there could not be a New Covenant.

The Apostle Paul told those at Thessalonica that the death of Jesus was part of the gospel (Acts 17:3). When confronted with those who attempted to place Christians back under the Law, Paul reminded those of the Galatian Church that they were not under the Law because Jesus was crucified (Galatians 3:1). Christians have been buried with Jesus, showing our complete death to that which once controlled us. Christians also have new life through His resurrection. This baptism into His death was not simply accounted to Christians but accomplished through the circumcision of the heart performed by the Holy Spirit (Romans 4:11; Colossians 2:11–12).

What role does the Holy Spirit play in a Christian's relationship to sin? This is one of many things that make Christians different from non-believers, who have a much different relationship to sin than those justified and set free now have (2 Corinthians 5:17). Non-believers can't help but sin, but believers have the power of the indwelling Holy Spirit not to sin, which means that Christians have died to sin's power (Colossians 3:3–5).

2) Read Romans 6:5–7

a) Verse 5: How have Christians been united with Christ?

b) Verse 6: What was crucified with Christ?

c) Verse 6: What is the result?

d) Verse 6: What are Christians no longer slaves to?

e) Verse 7: What must one do to be ultimately free from sin?

Paul tells how believers have been united with Christ in His death and resurrection. This means Christians are now dead to the Law, which is how sin gets its power (1 Corinthians 15:56). Non-believers are slaves to sin, while those justified are free from sin and its power. God calls the Law the ministry of death (2 Corinthians 3:7) and condemnation (2 Corinthinans 3:9). He also states that those under the Law are cursed (Galatians 3:10–11). The Law cannot bring life but only death (Galatians 3:21). Jesus expressed this truth when He told how everyone is a slave to sin and that only He could set them free (John 8:31–36).

How did Jesus set us free? Through His death and resurrection.

Those who teach that man is basically good and can somehow qualify himself for eternal life by obeying God's Commandments couldn't be more wrong. Those who teach these things are themselves slaves to sin. The devil wants this heresy taught, as he knows those under the Law are his. God is very clear that only those who have died are free from sin. This explains why Christians are so different and why a full immersion baptism best exemplifies what has happened in the life of a Christian. Notice how Paul refers to our old self being crucified with Jesus.

What do we know about the old self? We were concerned about the things of the flesh, slaves to sin, feared death (Hebrews 2:15), and were enemies of God (Romans 5:10).

How were we set free? By dying. This is so simple to understand: mankind needs to die in order to be free from sin's power. There are only two ways this can happen. One way is to die and face judgment. The other is to commit yourself to Jesus, being baptized into His death and resurrection, with the result of being set free. Those who do so are described as a new creation (Colossians 3:10; Ephesians 4:24).

3) Read Romans 6:8–11

a) Verse 8: How do those who died with Christ now live?

b) Verse 9: What truth are we told about Christ?

c) Verse 9: What does this mean for Christians?

d) Verse 10: What did Jesus die for?

e) Verse 10: What are we told about the life He now lives?

f) Verse 11: How does this apply to Christians?

Have you ever wondered what it will be like to die? If you have committed your life to Jesus, the answer is you already have. Did you feel anything? It will be the same when we leave this earth, as we will step out of our bodies. Since Christians have died with Christ, they will neither die again nor experience the agony that death brings (Acts 2:24). Since our old self died (Colossians 2:12), we have a new self that now lives for the glory of God (Ephesians 4:24; Colossians 3:10).

The finished work of Jesus included not only dying for sin but also to sin once and for all (Hebrews 10:10). Thus, He never has to die again. Jesus has done everything necessary for our salvation. This means that religious doctrines about practices like masses, holy days, prayers, confessions, and abstaining from food are not necessary and are, in fact, worthless in the battle against sin (Colossians 2:23).

In direct opposition to what God plainly states, the Catholic Church insists on a mass where Jesus is re-sacrificed. It states that the sacrifice of the mass is identical to the sacrifice of Christ (Catechism 1367), the mass is a bloodless sacrifice (Catechism 1367, 1382) offered for the living and the dead in order to obtain spiritual benefits from God (Catechism 1414), redemption is carried out by the mass (Catechism 1364), and the sacrifice of the mass is propitiatory (Catechism 1367).

Ask yourself these questions.

- *Does Jesus have to die again (or repeatedly)?*

- *Is His original sacrifice on the cross sufficient, or is more needed?*

- *Is God not clear about the sufficiency of Christ's death?*

- *Whom do I choose to place my faith in, God or man-made religion?*

Paul tells how the new life that Christians have been given enables them to live for God. That is, we have been set free so we can please and glorify God. Paul tells the opposite of what some were claiming and teaching (Romans 6:1): Christians (described as "in Christ") are to count themselves dead to sin and alive to God. Focusing on the fact that we have a different relationship with sin and death should be a daily ritual for all Christians. Know that all Christians have been empowered to say no to sin.

4) Read Romans 6:12–14

    a) Verse 12: How does one apply what we have just learned?

    b) Verse 13: What are Christians told to do?

    c) Verse 14: Can sin be a master over a Christian?

    d) Verse 14: Why not?

    e) Verse 14: What are Christians under?

    f) Verse 14: What are non-Christians under?

Notice how Paul implores us not to let sin reign in our mortal body; this is because it cannot reign in our spiritual body, which has been clothed with the righteousness of Jesus Christ (Romans 5:17–18). While on this earth, Christians live in a mortal body (1 Corinthians 15:44), but we also have a spiritual body that is one with Christ (1 Corinthians 12:27). Know that sin uses the flesh that has lusts and desires, and which wars with the indwelling Holy Spirit (Galatians 5:16; 1 Peter 2:11).

Paul wants Christians to know and apply the truth that we have died and been raised with Christ by not letting sin reign in their flesh. Christians have been empowered to refuse temptation (1 Corinthians 10:13). Through Jesus, all Christians have the victory over sin that the world lacks (1 Corinthians 15:57; 1 John 5:4).

How do we refuse temptation? By acknowledging every day that we are dead to sin's power and presenting our bodies to God as instruments of righteousness (Romans 12:1). God tells us to resist the devil (James 4:7), flee from lust (2 Timothy 2:22), and pursue righteousness (1 Timothy 6:11; 2 Timothy 2:22). This should be the daily intention of every Christian.

During communion, Christians should remind themselves that they are proclaiming not only the eternal benefits of Christ's death and resurrection—such as eternal life—but also the daily, present blessings that come with faith. These include being declared righteous by a holy God, having the Holy Spirit within us, access to God through Jesus, peace and joy in trials, and freedom from sin—privileges that non-Christians do not share.

We are told that non-Christians present their bodies as instruments of unrighteousness. This is natural for those "in the flesh" because sin is a master over those under the Law. This confirms that those under the Law are under the power of sin (1 Corinthians 15:56) and can only be set free through Jesus (John 8:36). Christians are baptized into Christ's death; thus, they are dead to sin (1 John 3:9, 5:18). The result is that Christians are not under God's Law (Galatians 5:18), but under grace (Romans 5:2).

Why is this so important to know that Christians have been set free from the Law? Because the devil wants people to remain slaves to sin and will attack Christians by trying to place them back under the Law. Paul dealt with this issue in the Galatian Church by reminding them of Christ's death (Galatians 3:1–10) and the curse of being under the Law. He also warned those who want to return under the Law that Christ will be of no advantage to them (Galatians 5:1–2).

We must balance this truth with the fact that the Law is holy and good (1 Timothy 1:8) and does not cause people to sin. It was a tutor to Christ (Galatians 3:24), as it closed every mouth by revealing what sin was and what sinners we were (Romans 3:19-20). The Jews did not understand this essential truth and responded to it by stoning Stephen (Acts 6:13) because they assumed he was preaching against the Law. Paul was also hated for the same reason (Acts 21:28). The absolute truth is that mankind has two options: submit to sin (remain under the Law) and die, or accept the gift of God (through Jesus) and live.

Verses 15–23

Paul reminds Christians what they were and who they are now.

5) Read Romans 6:15–16

a) Verse 15: What question does Paul ask?

b) Verse 15: What is the answer?

c) Verse 16: What happens to those who are slaves to sin?

d) Verse 16: What happens to those who are slaves to obedience?

Paul answered a question earlier concerning continuing in sin (Romans 6:1), and he now asks if we are free to sin because we are not under the Law but under grace. The clear answer is no. Notice how we are told that there are now two groups of people in this world: those under the Law and those under grace.

Ask yourself these questions:

- *Which group am I in?*

- *Have I been set free from sin?*

- *Do I reckon myself as dead to sin?*

If the answer is, "I don't know," then commit yourself to Jesus Christ and be set free. Remember, those under God's Law still face death and the judgment that follows (Hebrews 9:27), and at that time, death will have a sting (1 Corinthians 15:56).

Paul tells how people cannot serve two masters (Matthew 6:24; James 4:4). The one who presents himself to God should also intend to obey Him. Those who dedicate themselves to sin will suffer death (Romans 5:12), while those who present themselves to obedience will practice increased righteousness, eventually permeating their entire character. This is the process of sanctification.

One significant benefit of justification is the continual process of sanctification. Christians first have the intention to do God's will and then act on it by presenting themselves to God as an instrument of righteousness (Romans 6:13). Realize that this sanctification is a life-long process, while justification happens only once (Romans 5:1). We are told how the saved individual is first declared righteous by God and then willingly participates in being made into the image of Jesus (2 Corinthians 3:18; Colossians 3:10).

Why don't the unsaved have the ability to obey even if they intend to? Because there is no freedom from sin for those under God's Law.

6) Read Romans 6:17–18

a) Verse 17: How are non-Christians described?

b) Verse 17: What is the source of obedience for Christians?

c) Verse 18: What have Christians been freed from?

d) Verse 18: What are Christians now slaves to?

Christians should rejoice that though we were slaves to sin, we are now obedient to the *'form of teaching'* (Greek *tupos,* which means *'an impression or stamp'*) to which we are now committed.

What are Christians now obedient to? Paul means not the Law but the Christian doctrine the Holy Spirit has molded into us. Something much greater than the Law.

Christians are not only free from sin but also slaves to righteousness. This describes how Christians should live their life. While it is impossible for non-Christians to obey God, Christians are expected to obey God. Their obedience is due to the empowering work of the Holy Spirit, who makes it easy because, unlike the Law, which only tells you what not to do, the ministry of the Spirit changes your heart so you no longer want to sin (Psalm 51:10). This again shows the superiority of the new covenant over the Law (Ezekiel 36:26–27; Jeremiah 31:33).

God states that man is not able to cleanse himself from sin (Jeremiah 2:22). Religion denies this critical truth by teaching just the opposite, exhorting its followers to obey God, and when they fail to "get up, clean yourself off, and try again." The result is one who might think they are clean (Proverbs 30:12) but are filthy before a perfect God. Contrast this with the gospel, which states righteousness is impossible without Jesus (Matthew 19:25–26), but is a free gift only available with Jesus.

We should now understand that there are two distinct groups of people on this earth. Look at some of the differences:

<u>**Non-Christians Under the Law**</u>

in Adam (1 Corinthians 15:22)
slaves to sin (Romans 6:14; 1 Corinthians 15:56)
sinful nature (Romans 6:13)
on their way to hell (Matthew 23:33)
good deeds are filthy rags (Isaiah 64:6)

<u>**Christians Under Grace**</u>

in Christ (1 Corinthians 1:30)
freed from sin (Romans 6:7)
slave to righteousness (Romans 6:18)
eternal life in heaven (John 3:16)
have Christ's righteousness (Romans 5:17)

Imagine the Law as a set of bars separating the two groups of people. Those under the Law look through the bars with the distorted view that Christians are behind them when, in reality, it is the non-Christians who are behind the bars (under God's Law) looking out at those who Jesus has freed. Non-Christians view Christians as being under the yoke of the Law, not understanding they are the ones in slavery. The world views Christianity as being under God's Law, not understanding the reality that Christians are free and changed and do not want to participate in "worldly behavior" and the baggage that comes with it.

7) Read Romans 6:19–20

a) Verse 19: What did Christians do before they put their faith in Christ?

b) Verse 19: What was the result?

c) Verse 19: What are Christians instructed to do now?

d) Verse 19: What is the result?

e) Verse 20: What is an unsaved person free from?

Paul used the analogy of slavery to help the people understand the advantages those saved and justified now have. We are told how those who present themselves as slaves to impurity and lawlessness experience a downward spiral that results in further lawlessness. Christians present themselves as instruments of righteousness, which results in their sanctification. Notice how this work does not result in justification, which happens once at the time of salvation. This process is an integral part of our sanctification. While the Holy Spirit does the work, Christians are implored to pursue their sanctification (Hebrews 12:14). Because God gives believers a new heart, this should be a deliberate action.

Remember how we used to run after sin? That is precisely how every believer should pursue their sanctification. We have discussed how only Christians are righteous before a holy God. Paul tells how the unsaved are free regarding any righteousness—a false freedom because they can't be righteous. Know that this applies to everyone, including the religious leaders like priests, pastors, and the Pharisees, who Jesus described as whitewashed tombs (Matthew 23:27). Jesus described the sin of self-righteousness (Luke 18:9–14), teaching that arrogance will be humbled while humility will be rewarded.

Compare this with the Catholic Church (Catechism 773), which teaches that "The Church's structure is totally ordered to the holiness of Christ's members." This claims that the pope, then the cardinals, then the bishops, and then the priests are all holier than the people. Isn't it amazing how easily the masses accept this heresy? Ignorance of God's Word is what allows this to happen.

I know that as a result of putting my complete faith in Jesus, I have been clothed with the righteousness of Jesus Christ! We can now better understand Paul's witness that the only righteousness he had was given to him as a result of his faith (Philippians 3:9). Unlike a group of religious leaders who essentially state that "I am righteous because I say so," Christians can state that "I am righteous because God says so." Only God's opinion matters!

8) Read Romans 6:21–23

a) Verse 21: What question is asked?

b) Verse 21: What is your answer?

c) Verse 21: What is the fruit of sin?

d) Verse 22: Who are Christians enslaved to?

e) Verse 22: What is the result?

f) Verse 23: What is the wage of one's sin?

g) Verse 23: What is the free gift of God?

h) Verse 23: Who is this only available through?

Paul asks a profound question concerning sin: Exactly what did my previous life of sin get me? The answer is shame and death. Think about the many different types of sin. Do they not destroy those who partake in them?

Now, ask yourself these questions:

- *Do I now see how sin has impacted my life?*

- *Do I want this to continue?*

- *Has not God clearly shown me that in Christ, I am free and can live an obedient life before Him?*

- *Do I believe it?*

We can now better understand how God wants us to daily reckon ourselves dead to sin and alive to Him (Romans 6:11). I thank God for what He has saved me from, things that I am now ashamed of ever doing. Ultimately, the only benefit of sin is shame and death, and it shows its true colors by how it destroys people's lives. The good news is that Christians are now slaves to righteousness, with the result being holiness and God's promise of eternal life (1 John 2:25).

IF THE GOSPEL WERE CONDENSED INTO ONE SENTENCE, ROMANS 6:23 WOULD BE IT!

Since perfection is needed for eternal life, the wages of even one simple sin is death. Just as Moses declared in setting life and death before the people (Deuteronomy 30:19), mankind has a decision to make: earn the wages of sin (death) or accept the free gift of God through Jesus Christ (life).

In this chapter, Paul stresses that we should apply the knowledge of the benefits of our justification to our actions. The result should be reckoning ourselves dead to sin and presenting ourselves to God as slaves to righteousness. The result will be obedience and our progressive sanctification.

CHAPTER SEVEN

The relationship a Christian has to the Law.

Verses 1–6

Paul now explains a Christian's relationship with God's Law.

1) Read Romans 7:1–4

a) Verse 1: How long does the Law have jurisdiction over someone?

b) Verse 2: What analogy does Paul use to show this?

c) Verses 3 & 4: What happens to the married woman if her husband dies?

d) Verse 4: How do Christians die to the Law?

e) Verse 4: To whom are we now joined?

f) Verse 4: What is the result?

Paul previously discussed the believer's relationship to sin; he now discusses the believer's relationship to the Law. You might be thinking, have we not discussed how those under the Law are cursed (Galatians 3:10–11), and how it is called the ministry of death and condemnation (2 Corinthians 3:7–9)? Now we are told that everyone is under the Law as long as he or she lives? I thought Christians were free. Did Paul not just state Christians have been crucified with Christ (Romans 6:8), and are not under the Law (Romans 6:14)? How can this be reconciled? Paul explains this by using the analogy of the civil laws of marriage, in which you are bound to your spouse while they are alive, and if one dies, you are free to marry another.

Those who have died are free (Romans 6:7), while those who are alive (non-believers) remain bound to the Law. The application of this truth is that those baptized into the death of Jesus are dead to the Law, which only has jurisdiction as long as one lives (Colossians 1:22). Christians no longer have a relationship with the Law, but rather one with Christ! Let me repeat: Christians have nothing to do with the Law anymore. We had to die to sin in order to be joined to Christ.

God has done things this way so Christians can bear fruit for God. Jesus referred to this important truth, telling how unless something dies, it cannot bear fruit (John 12:24). The Apostle Paul also confirmed this fact to the Corinthian Church (1 Corinthians 15:36). The result is a new life (in Christ) that allows us to bear fruit for God (John 15:1–5), thus bringing Him glory (John 15:8).

2) Read Romans 7:5–6

a) Verse 5: How are non-Christians described?

b) Verse 5: What does the Law arouse?

c) Verse 5: What is the result?

d) Verse 6: What have Christians been released from?

e) Verse 6: How did it happen?

f) Verse 6: In what ways do Christians now serve?

g) Verse 6: How is the Law described?

We are once again shown how non-Christians (unsaved) are considered "in the flesh." Notice how the Law arouses sinful passions—God's righteous standards provoke a rebellious response. This does not happen to Christians who are "in the spirit" (Romans 8:9).

Can a Christian ever be "in the flesh?" No, they can act like it by chasing after things of the flesh, but they can never return. Christians have died to the flesh, sin (Romans 6:1–6), and the Law, which no longer has dominion over them.

Once we know this truth, the natural follow-up question is, can a Christian be a slave to sin? While it might appear so, the answer is no. How can you live in something to which you died (Romans

6:2)? While a Christian can give in to the desires of the flesh and live a sinful life, it is impossible for a Christian to be a slave to sin. The reason is that they have died through the circumcision of the Spirit and have been placed into the body of Christ. Know that this circumcision of the heart cannot be undone.

What about Christians who seem to be slaves to sin? If they choose to sin and yet are not disciplined by God, they are not who they claim to be. Apparent slavery to sin at some point may indicate the person wasn't a believer in the first place. God promises discipline to those who disobey and says those who sin without His discipline are not genuine believers (Hebrews 12:6–10).

Do Christians continue to sin? Yes, while on this earth, they still walk in their flesh, which has sinful desires (1 John 1:8; 2 Corinthians 10:3; 1 John 2:16). While sin continues to influence, it can no longer enslave. That is why we are told to reckon ourselves as dead to sin (Romans 6:11) and yield ourselves to God by walking by the Spirit (Galatians 5:16–17) and not giving in to the desires of the flesh (Ephesians 2:3). Know that this is a deliberate, on-going, daily action.

You might ask: Is it even possible to go back? No! Is it possible to remarry a deceased spouse? Remember, the Law only has authority over those still alive. Christians have been released from the Law, which remains in effect. Christians have died to the Law and now serve another, who is Jesus Christ. The result is that Christians are slaves to righteousness (Romans 6:19). Remember, Christians are alive in the Spirit (Romans 2:29), not under the letter of the Law, which kills (2 Corinthians 3:6). The Spirit gives life. This is much different from the "legalism" that many religions dictate.

Does this mean Christians are not under any law? Are we free to sin? No! We are now under the law of Christ, which Paul will discuss in Chapter Twelve (Galatians 6:2).

Verses 7–14

The Law is the ministry of death, which defines sin and also reveals
its true nature and terrible effect on the sinner.

3) Read Romans 7:7–8

a) Verse 7: What question is asked?

b) Verse 7: What is the answer?

c) Verse 7: What does the Law do?

d) Verse 7: What sin is mentioned by Paul as an example?

e) Verse 8: What did the Law do?

f) Verse 8: Where is sin without the Law?

We have talked at length about the Law, and you might wonder, is it bad? Is the Law sin? Is it to blame for my death? God's answer is no! The Law is holy and perfect (Psalm 19:7). Sin is evil, and this important truth is only revealed and defined by the Law.

Notice how sin uses the Law to produce coveting of every kind. As Paul discovered personally, the sin of being covetous is the root of many other sins. In many cases, it is idolatry itself (Ephesians 5:5). This was exemplified when a wealthy young man asked Jesus what was necessary for eternal life (Matthew 19:16–22). Jesus told him to obey the commandments (of course, He meant perfectly, challenging the man's self-righteousness). When the young man told Jesus how he had done so, the Lord instructed him to sell his possessions and follow. He left grieving because he coveted material things, being guilty of the last Commandment (Exodus 20:17).

The Bible gives many examples of coveting leading to sin:

- Eve first coveted and then ate the forbidden fruit (Genesis 3:6).

- Achan coveted and took things under the ban (Joshua 7) (robe, silver, and gold), resulting in judgment for him and his family.

- David coveted Bathsheba and sinned (2 Samuel 11).

- Ahab coveted Naboth's vineyard, resulting in his wife Jezebel conspiring to have Naboth killed (1 Kings 21).

- Judas sold Jesus for thirty pieces of silver (Matthew 26:15).

Since coveting is the root cause of many other sins, it is easier to understand why God tells us to be content with what we have (Hebrews 13:5). Jesus warns us to be on our guard against every form of greed (Luke 12:15). Sin uses the Law to produce a greater desire to do what is commanded not to do. Without the Law, sin is dead, not known for what it is.

Does this mean there was no sin before the Law? No, there was sin, but it was not fully shown to be sin until it was defined by the Law (Romans 3:20, 5:12–13). Until that point, what was operating ineffectively was the "law written on the heart" (Romans 2:14–16), the conscience they ignored. For instance, God says not to steal (Exodus 20:15), confirming the widely held standard that one ought not to take what belongs to someone else, illustrated several times in the life of Abraham (Genesis 12:17–18, 14:21–24, 23:7–14). Once the Law was given, when one steals, they do not meet the standard that God set in His Law.

This is why sin is defined as actually falling short of the standards that God has set. The Greek word for *'sin'* is *hamartia*, which literally means *'missing the mark.'* Man's rightful place before a perfect God is only accomplished by comparing their life to the standards He has set.

4) Read Romans 7:9–11

a) Verse 9: What happens when the Law reveals unrighteousness?

b) Verse 9: What caused Paul to die?

c) Verse 10: What is erroneously thought that the Law brings?

d) Verse 10: What does the Law bring?

e) Verse 11: What did sin do?

Before his conversion, Paul thought himself alive and well because he mistakenly believed that the Law established his righteousness (Philippians 3:6). Paul was unaware that the Law had condemned him (John 5:45). He was also unaware of the Law's effect on his relationship to sin. When the truth was revealed to Paul (1 Timothy 1:15), he realized he was spiritually dead (Ephesians 2:5; Colossians 2:13). Not understanding the Law (and its purpose) can cause one to think they are alive and righteous before God. Know that this is the mindset of most "religious" people. Instead of bringing life, the Law shows that we are dead to righteousness and without hope.

Imagine the Law as a mirror that reveals our blemishes (James 1:22–25). Could we see our blemishes without the mirror? Does the revealing of our blemishes make the mirror bad? Of course not! The Law is good, but it reveals sin. Know that the Law and sin are different in that the Law is the standard, while sin is the failure to meet it.

All Christians were at one time deceived by sin (Titus 3:3), but how does sin deceive? By promising satisfaction and happiness (Genesis 3:13) and by also hiding the horrendous effects it brings on people (Hebrews 3:13). The result is individuals who are slaves to sin and consumed with a life of sin which is not selective as to whose life it destroys (2 Peter 2:14). Sin is like a disease that runs rampant eventually consuming everything. When sin is accomplished, it brings death (James 1:15) and the sting that comes with it (1 Corinthians 15:56).

Was the Law was ever intended to give life? Of course not! While the Jews might have thought so, they should have realized that the Law has no provisions for worship and certainly none for eternal life. Everyone is born into this world not only guilty (Romans 5:11–4) but also without the righteousness of Jesus Christ that is needed for access to the Father (Ephesians 2:18, 3:12). There are many religions today that still erroneously teach that the Law (or laws of their own making) brings life, not knowing that being under it ensures death (Romans 6:23).

5) Read Romans 7:12–14

a) Verse 12: How is the Law described?

b) Verse 13: Did the Law cause your death?

c) Verse 13: What did sin do?

d) Verse 13: What does this reveal about sin?

e) Verse 14: What truth does Paul reaffirm?

f) Verse 14: To what is our flesh sold into bondage?

After earlier clarifying the point that the Law is not sin, Paul now states the Law is holy, righteous, and good (Psalm 19:7; 1 Timothy 1:8). The Law did not cause our death, sin did (Romans 6:23). God's holy Law declared us dead and, like a doctor, signed our death certificate. God used the Law to reveal the true destructive nature of sin. Few understand how sin destroys people's lives. Sinning will always lead to disgrace (Proverbs 14:34). I have witnessed sin destroy families, relationships, and careers, and even cause death in individuals.

Before redemption, all Christians were held under bondage to sin (Galatians 4:3), but how did we get there? Through the sin of Adam and confirmation by the Law (Romans 5:12–14). Paul repeats how the Law is spiritual as he is about to talk about how it affects people. He makes this point because he does not want anyone to wrongly perceive that the Law was the cause of our death. Sin is what killed us.

Unlike living under the Law (which is spiritual and holy), Christians are still living in their body, the flesh, which (being corrupted with a sinful nature) wants to sin. Many Christians fail to understand the true nature of their flesh and its sinful desires. Because of their inherited sinful nature, people are much different than the holy and sinless Law. The Law cannot change you or even empower you to be good. This is exemplified by the fact that the flesh (with its desires) will always war against our spirit. This battle is evident to Christians, who have been revealed the true nature of their flesh.

When did Christians become aware of the carnality of their flesh? Through the circumcision of the heart that the Holy Spirit performed. This spiritual circumcision separates a believer's flesh from their spirit (Colossians 2:11–13) and places them into the Body of Christ. This also results in life and freedom from the Law, which they are now dead to.

Because Christians were formerly sold to sin through the sin of Adam, they will face a daily battle with the desires of the flesh to sin (Galatians 2:20). Because we are alive in Christ though still living in the flesh, examples of this ongoing battle between our flesh and spirit include hunger, a drive for sex, drugs or alcohol, and other natural or unnatural desires. In addition, Christians still have to battle the lusts of the pride of life (1 John 2:16). We earlier discussed how coveting is the root of most sins. God tells us how the world is corrupted by lust (2 Peter 1:4), which gives birth to sin (James 1:15). The key point is that Christians have been equipped to fight this battle by the indwelling Holy Spirit. Because Christians are not of this world (John 18:36), they are expected to obey God (1 Peter 1:1–2).

◆ ◆ ◆

Verses 15–25

Paul describes the battle with the flesh he still lives in and the relationship Christians have with it.

6) Read Romans 7:15–16

a) Verse 15: How does Paul describe the battle within him?

b) Verse 15: How did Paul describe sinning?

c) Verse 16: What did sinning against his own will reveal?

While Paul knew he was a sinner, don't read this and make the mistake of thinking of him as still a wretched slave to sin. In earlier epistles, he had stated that he was not conscious of anything against himself (1 Corinthians 4:4) and had conducted himself in holiness and godly sincerity. He also kept a watchful eye on his conscience (2 Corinthians 1:12; 1 Timothy 1:5, 19; 2 Timothy 1:3).

Paul is talking about the battle between his flesh and spirit, which is something all Christians can identify with. Paul wanted to obey but failed, describing his sins as something he hated, a response many non-believers would not typically voice. This fact describes one of the changes that regeneration brings, as Christians will generally want to obey, while non-Christians will typically want to sin. The point is that Paul (just like all Christians) became aware of this battle when he became free from the Law.

Realize that the battle itself is evidence of salvation. Paul explains that his quandary was not the result of his misunderstanding or having a wrong attitude toward the Law. Like all Christians, Paul realized that being alive in his flesh meant he would experience the battle he described.

Why can't Christians practice sin (Colossians 3:9; 1 John 3:8–9)? Because they can't live in something they died to (Romans 6:2) and have been freed from (Romans 6:7, 17, 22). That being said, there is still a battle that happens in the life of a Christian (Galatians 5:17). Paul tells us how even though we are not under the Law, we still walk in the flesh (2 Corinthians 10:3). That is, our spirits still live in our bodies. The fact that Paul knew sinning was terrible confirmed that the Law is good.

7) Read Romans 7:17–18

a) Verse 17: What does the Law reveal?

b) Verse 18: What does Paul say about his flesh?

c) Verse 18: What did Paul's spirit want to do?

d) Verse 18: Did Paul's spirit always win the battle?

The Law reveals how sin is alive and present within our flesh. All Christians experience an intense battle between their flesh and spirit. Paul concluded that nothing good dwelt in his flesh, which has a sinful nature. Before being saved, believers were one with their flesh, with the result that their flesh and its sinful desires ruled their spirit. They were individuals described as being "in the flesh." Christians are now "in the spirit." Like Paul, Christians are set free from their flesh yet still battle against its strong desires (John 3:6). We must keep in mind that even amid the battle, our spirits have been clothed with the righteousness of Jesus (Ephesians 4:24).

8) Read Romans 7:19–22

a) Verse 19: What does Paul not do?

b) Verses 20 & 21: What conclusion did Paul come to

c) Verse 22: What did Paul's spirit want to do?

Paul tells how he wanted to obey but still sinned. This is no different from any Christian who, even though set free from the power of sin, still fails. Let me again state that while no one born of God practices sin (1 John 3:9), they will experience a battle against their flesh as long as they are alive in the flesh. Paul concludes that his flesh wants to sin, but his real self, which is his spirit (which rejoices in the Law), does not. Paul tells how the source of sin in a Christian is their flesh.

Does this mean that Christians are not accountable for their sin? God forbid! Know that while not affecting their right standing with God, sin has consequences for a Christian.

The early church had to deal with the extreme teaching that it was alright for a Christian to sin because it was their flesh sinning. This was based on the idea that the human body itself was evil and even led to some promoting a theology that Jesus did not come in a human body because that would have automatically implicated Him in sin. The conclusion that sins of the flesh didn't matter is so wrong because Christians, while still living in this world, should avoid sin at all costs (Romans 6:2). This is because sin can have destructive consequences, and God will discipline His children when they sin (Hebrews 12:5–6). While there is a continuous struggle between the flesh and the indwelling Spirit in a believer (Galatians 5:16–18), their new nature is evidence of their salvation (2 Corinthians 5:17).

9) Read Romans 7:23–25

a) Verse 23: What kind of law is working in Paul's flesh?

b) Verse 23: What is the result?

c) Verse 24: What important question is asked?

d) Verse 25: What is the answer?

e) Verse 25: What battle does every Christian face?

While Paul's spirit joyfully concurs with obeying God's Law (Romans 7:22), he tells how he is a prisoner of a different law (one of the flesh) that is at war against his will. The result is a state he described as being a prisoner. This again shows the weakness of the Law, as it cannot free one from sin or deliver us from our sinful nature. This is only accomplished through the Law of the Spirit, which brings freedom and changes our attitude toward sin (Ezekiel 36:27).

Even after being saved, Paul recognized that every Christian experiences a daily battle. While Christians have been given victory, it is important to know they have been equipped for their battle with God's Word, which, when read, not only cleanses (John 17:17; Ephesians 5:26) but also prevents one from sinning (Psalm 119:9). In describing this battle, Paul talks about the Law of God and the law of sin.

What is the difference between the Law of God and the law of sin? We know that the Law of God is spiritual, and the law of sin is the fact that our flesh has been sold into bondage to sin (Romans 7:14, 23).

This is why Paul can state that Christians are the true circumcision who now put no confidence in the flesh (Philippians 3:3). Notice how Paul declares he can only be set free by the Lord Jesus Christ. This shows the intentional place that Jesus should have in every believer's thinking and living. The battle that Paul describes is one that every believer experiences. Paul was not describing himself before he was saved. All Christians will one day be freed of this battle by Jesus, either at their death or the rapture.

❖ ❖ ❖

The key point in this chapter is that it is all about the life of the Spirit. While still living in the corrupt flesh, Christians will never totally attain the place they want to be.

Does the battle between our flesh and our spirit mean we should not even attempt to change? Absolutely not! God says our sanctification is His will (1 Thessalonians 4:3) and instructs all Christians to pursue their sanctification (Hebrews 12:14).

We can claim for ourselves the sentiment Paul expressed in Philippians 2:13 (ESV), "It is God who works in you, both to will and to work for his good pleasure." Paul is describing something that I have experienced. Before committing my life to Jesus, I knew the difference between right and wrong, yet I was a slave to sin. While keenly aware I would one day have to answer for my sins, I felt little or no remorse when I did sin.

Even though I felt accused and condemned, these feelings did nothing to change me or my attitude toward sin. Let me repeat: I was enslaved to sin. How did I deal with my sin? I went to confession, which I wrongly thought would somehow erase my sins and qualify me for eternal life. Any contrition I felt was only due to the consequences of my sin, not the fact that it was wrong and offended God.

As a Christian, I now face the battle Paul describes daily. When I do sin, I almost immediately feel remorse, usually get on my knees, confess to my Lord that what I did was wrong, and ask for His forgiveness. This is completely different from what I used to do and feel. I now confess my sins, not to escape their eternal consequences, but as part of my sanctification, acknowledging my wrongdoing and asking Jesus to change me.

Let me point out how the Holy Spirit plays an important role in this process by "convicting" yet not "condemning" me for my sin. Unlike before being saved, I now want to do what is right and feel convicted when I don't. This truth sets the stage for what I believe is the most important chapter in the Bible, where Paul expounds on the victory that has been given to all Christians.

CHAPTER EIGHT

The differences between a Christian and a non-believer.

This chapter might be the most important one in Paul's letter. Here, the Apostle puts the final piece of the argument about what makes the Gospel the expression of God's power for salvation (Romans 1:16). It begins with no condemnation and ends with no separation for the believer.

◆ ◆ ◆

Verses 1–4

Paul now explains the state of a believer.

1) Read Romans 8:1

a) What blessing is described?

b) Who alone can claim this benefit?

c) What does the Greek word for condemnation mean?

d) What does this truth mean to you?

Paul closed Chapter Seven, describing the battle with the flesh that all Christians endure. He now encourages them with the term "therefore," showing the resulting state a believer now lives in. Because the previous chapter is true, there is now no condemnation for those "in Christ Jesus." Notice how this benefit only comes to those who are "in Christ," that is, those in whom Christ lives (Romans 8:9). Consider that the first verse of this chapter might be one of the most important in the entire Bible (Romans 8:1). It declares a blessing that all Christians have.

No condemnation is a truth that many fail to accept. Those who disagree will call this "cheap grace."

That accusation fails to appreciate the depth and cost contained in the phrase "in Christ Jesus." The Greek word for *'condemnation'* is *katakrima,* which means *'penalty.'* There is no penalty for the sin of Christians; this is because Jesus paid their penalty of death on the cross (Ezekiel 18:4; Romans 6:23). Think about this statement. Christians have no penalty for their sins because Jesus already paid it for them (Mark 10:25; 1 Timothy 2:5).

One application of this truth is the fact that Christians are eternally secure. Another is that the Holy Spirit will never condemn but rather convict a believer of sin. If you are still having a hard time digesting this good news, take a moment and think about the other blessed truths of the gospel, which tells how Jesus took our sins upon Himself on the cross (Isaiah 53) and how He has clothed Christians with His righteousness (Isaiah 61:10; Romans 5:17–18). The gospel is truly good news.

Does this mean Christians are free to sin? God forbid! Paul already dealt with this ridiculous question (Romans 6). The last chapter told how the inner man will not want to sin, and while Christians will continue to sin, they have a different relationship to sin than they had before becoming saved. That being said, while not affecting our legal standing with God, sin still has destructive consequences in the life of a Christian, who, while free from the Great White Throne judgment (Revelation 20:11–12), will still partake in the Bema judgment (2 Corinthians 5:10).

Does this promise of no condemnation apply only to past sins? No, it applies to all sins, including those not yet committed.

Ask yourself these questions:

* *Do I believe God when He states that everyone's sin was placed on Jesus at the cross (Isaiah 53:6; 1 Peter 2:24)?*

* *Do I believe God who states that Jesus paid the price of death for our sins (Isaiah 53:12; 1 Corinthians 15:3)?*

* *Is God not clear on this subject?*

Why do I ask this series of questions? Because the present-day church in Rome (Catholic) teaches that there is condemnation, which will be paid for in Purgatory. Know that one must disregard Scripture to teach and believe there is a place of fire called Purgatory that is necessary to atone for sin and cleanse the soul (Catechism 1031). The Catechism (1472) also states that one must be purified from sin in Purgatory, which must be accepted as a grace (1473). Once we compare this teaching with the truth of Scripture, we know that nothing could be further from the truth. The doctrine of Purgatory disregards a huge part of the gospel and actually makes God out to be a liar (1 John 5:10).

Know that the doctrine of Purgatory is the main source of the wealth of the Church in Rome. How? By selling (through masses) the indulgences needed so their loved ones can be set free. This disregards the fact that God plainly states that no man can redeem his brother (Psalm 49:7), and only the blood of Jesus can cleanse from sin (1 John 1:7).

2) Read Romans 8:2–4

    a) Verse 2: What has the Law of the Spirit set us free from?

    b) Verse 2: What did the law of sin bring us?

    c) Verse 3: What are we told about the Law?

    d) Verse 3: What did God do?

    e) Verse 4: What did Jesus fulfill for us?

    f) Verse 4: How do Christians walk?

Paul now explains how Christians are set free from their body of death. Through the indwelling Holy Spirit (2 Corinthians 3:17), Christians have been set free from the law of sin and death, which no longer has power in the life of a Christian (Romans 7:24–25). The result is that the Law cannot condemn Christians. We earlier discussed how the Holy Spirit dwells in believers, giving them a new heart, which results in a changed attitude toward sin (Ezekiel 36:27).

The law of the Spirit is having faith in what the Almighty God has to say about the most important subject in our lives (Romans 3:25–27), with the result being justification. This law is superior to the Mosaic Law because it is not limited to working in our flesh. Even though the Law is holy and good, it could not deal with sin as the result of being under. It not only increased sin but also brought condemnation (John 5:45). It dealt with the flesh and not the root (and most important part) of the problem, which is our spirit.

The Law is described as weak and powerless (Hebrews 7:18); this is because it deals with those still "in the flesh," which has sinful desires that control the non-believer. The Law could not and did not deal with sin. Remember, the Law had no provisions for eternal life, could not make anyone righteous (Galatians 3:21), and could not change anyone. Contrast that with the fact that the Holy Spirit brings life, works internally, and frees us from sin and condemnation.

Knowing all this, God's eternal plan to defeat sin (Ephesians 3:11) was not through the Law (Acts 13:39; Hebrews 10:1) but rather through His Son Jesus Christ, who was a sin offering, thus condemning sin in the flesh. While Jesus was without sin (Hebrews 4:15), He came to this earth in the likeness of all men, fully capable of being tempted in all ways as we are (Philippians 2:7; Hebrews 2:14).

What do we know about the Old Testament sin offering (Leviticus 4)? It was an offering for sins that had been committed either in ignorance, inadvertently, or unintentionally. Unlike other types of sacrifices (except the guilt or trespass offering), the sin offering was not voluntary. Unlike other offerings, it was not a soothing aroma to the Lord. The priest would offer a bull (without defect) that had been killed at the doorway before the Lord. He would sprinkle the blood seven times before the veil and also take the blood and put it on the horns of the altar of incense, which was located before the veil in the Holy Place. He then took the blood and poured it out at the base of the altar of burnt offering. The fat, kidneys, and liver were then removed from the bull and offered to the Lord. The rest of the bull was taken outside the camp and burned.

Why was this important? Because it signified how Jesus was to be slain outside the Holy Place (Hebrews 13:12–13) and showed how Jesus would remove the sin from the people and make them holy. Remember, believers also leave the camp (the Law) to come to Jesus. This shows how one must leave the legalities of the Jewish faith in order to be saved. Christians do not walk according to the flesh because the Law no longer has jurisdiction over them (Romans 7:1).

According to Romans 8:4, are Christians are required or expected to fulfill the Law? The answer is that the requirement of the Law (perfection) has already been fulfilled in Christians by the indwelling Holy Spirit, who clothes us with the righteousness of Jesus Christ (Matthew 5:17). We have already discussed how no one can fulfill the Law. That is why everyone needs Jesus, who fulfilled the Law for everyone. The result of having the indwelling Spirit is an individual who is now considered "in the Spirit" and who will normally follow the leading of the Holy Spirit.

Does this mean Christians will always follow the leading of the Holy Spirit? The answer is, unfortunately, no. However, the Christian will not normally stray far from the Lord, as the Spirit will normally make His presence felt when one decides to give in to the desires of the flesh. Paul knew of this when he exhorted Christians to walk by the Spirit, which is akin to submitting and depending on Him in our daily battle with sin (Galatians 5:16). Know that this is a deliberate act.

Verse 5–7

The differences between those "in the flesh" and "those in the Spirit."

3) Read Romans 8:5–7

a) Verse 5: What do non-believers focus on?

b) Verse 5: What do Christians normally focus on?

c) Verse 6: What is the result for non-believers?

d) Verse 6: What is the result for Christians?

f) Verse 7: How are non-believers described?

g) Verse 7: Do they typically try to obey the Law?

h) Verse 7: Can a non-believer obey the Law?

Paul does not describe two different Christians but rather the major differences between Christians and non-Christians. Even if Christians periodically give in to the desires of their flesh, they are not living according to the flesh, as this title is for non-believers alone. Christians are living according to the Spirit! What is the difference? In a non-believer (under the Law), their spirit and their flesh are joined. This is the reason why the desires of the flesh rule.

The flesh has sinful desires and, when joined with one's spirit, will cause an individual to constantly set their minds on the things of the flesh. Normal desires of the flesh include things like sexual lust (Galatians 5:19–21), immorality, an appetite for alcohol or drugs, a prideful inner desire to be noticed, greed, jealousy, anger, and strife. The result for the non-believer is no hope (Ephesians 2:12) and eternal separation from God (1 Timothy 5:6).

The good news is that one can turn from the world to Christ and be saved from this hopeless state. Christians are now joined to God and can never be separated from Him (John 10:29). Due to the Holy Spirit circumcising the heart of believers (Colossians 2:11), their spirit is now separated from their sinful flesh and joined to the body of Christ (Romans 7:4). The result is that Christians are no longer one with their flesh, but rather one with the Lord.

This is the reason that Christians normally focus on the things of God (Galatians 5:22–25), while non-believers focus on the desires of the flesh (Ephesians 2:3). Paul is very straightforward in these verses. Those in the flesh are concerned with the flesh and not the things of God. They are hostile toward God and could not obey Him even if they wanted to (James 4:4).

This not only describes non-Christians, but it also addresses even those considered religious believers. Why do I state this? Because, just like I once was, millions of people would state they believe in Jesus but are under the Law, trying to obey God without the regeneration and power of the Holy Spirit in their lives.

The Catholic religion wrongly taught me that I had to obey the Law and that my relationship with God was based on how well I managed any disobedience. I was never taught that I had to commit my life and trust in Jesus. I was never taught I had to be born again (John 3:3–5). I was wrongly taught that I became a Christian when baptized as an infant. The result was an exercise in futility when trying to obey

God.

Take a moment and think about a dog chasing its tail. This is akin to trying to obey God without the circumcision performed by the indwelling Holy Spirit, which follows conversion. Know that the Word of God is very clear. No matter how good their intentions are, it is impossible for non-believers to obey God. It is only through Jesus that one can be set free from the power of sin (John 8:36).

◆ ◆ ◆

Verses 8–11

God's definition of a Christian.

4) Read Romans 8:8–11

a) Verse 8: What are we told about non-Christians?

b) Verse 9: What distinguishes a Christian?

c) Verse 9: Whom does a non-Christian not have?

d) Verse 10: How is the state of a Christian defined?

e) Verse 11: What does the indwelling Holy Spirit give?

We are told how non-believers cannot please God. Know that this includes millions of people who have been wrongly taught they are Christians. Man's definition of a Christian is anyone who simply states they believe in Jesus. What do we know about these people? They have never made a commitment of their faith to Jesus alone, and because of that fact, they lack the regeneration needed for eternal life.

Some translations wrongly change the literal phrase "in the flesh" that God uses in verses eight and nine. We have discussed how non-believers lack the circumcision of the spirit. Their spirits are one with their flesh. God describes them as being "in the flesh" (Romans 7:5). Many mistake the meaning of verse 8 as Paul talking about a Christian walking after the desires of the flesh rather than seeing that the Apostle is affirming that his readers have been made alive by God's Spirit and are dead to sin. Paul began this chapter by telling of the benefit of no condemnation for those "in Christ."

Paul now defines exactly who is "in Christ." This is so important because here God defines who the real Christians are!God's Word is clear. Those who reject the gospel of Jesus ("in the flesh") cannot please God. This includes people whom the world might even consider holy. Those in the flesh (uncircumcised in heart) cannot obey His Laws, are without His righteousness, and are concerned with the desires of their flesh and the things of the world (Philippians 3:19).

It is easy to see why they cannot please God. Those in the flesh could try to be perfect, help the poor, and lead a good life, but because of their lack of faith in Jesus, they would still fall far short of pleasing God. While some might outwardly appear to be holy, they would still be slaves to sin. This is a good Scripture to remember for those who will tell you that all it takes to get to Heaven is being a good person. God has told us that no one is righteous on their own (Romans 3:10, 23). Everyone needs a Savior, and we now know why this is so. Others will state that God will not allow so-called good people to go to hell. This Scripture certainly refutes that statement. Only Christians, please God. Only Christians have eternal life.

Remember, this letter was written to believers at the church in Rome. Paul encourages them by reminding them they can determine whether they are, in fact, a Christian. The test is whether the Holy Spirit dwells in you (2 Corinthians 13:5), as this is God's definition of a Christian. The Holy Spirit must live in you if you are to be called a Christian (1 Corinthians 3:16). This is what makes Christians so different!

Do you think that the God of the Bible could live in someone and not make a huge difference in their life (1 Corinthians 6:9–11)? Remember, He does not just sit there. He is a down payment for salvation (Ephesians 1:14); He seals us through circumcision (Ephesians 1:13); He clothes us with Christ's righteousness (which is the cause of our justification) (Romans 5:17–18), frees us from the Law and makes us holy through the process of sanctification (2 Thessalonians 2:13). The Holy Spirit also teaches and comforts us (John 14:26; 1 John 2:27) in our time of need (Acts 9:31).

Notice how God's Word interchanges the Holy Spirit with the Spirit of Christ (Romans 8:9–10). Luke also used the terms Holy Spirit and the Spirit of Jesus interchangeably when telling how both Paul and Timothy were led (Acts 16:6–7). These are the same Persons of the Trinity. Paul also reminds the believers that while our bodies are as good as dead, our spirits are alive and clothed with Christ's righteousness. We can be encouraged by the fact that the Holy Spirit will raise believers, just as He raised Jesus from the dead.

Verses 12–13

The application of the Holy Spirit within Christians.

5) Read Romans 8:12–13

a) Verse 12: How are Christians obligated not to live?

b) Verse 13: What are we told about those who live according to the flesh?

c) Verse 13: How are Christians to live?

d) Verse 13: What do Christians put to death?

After describing the differences between believers and non-believers, Paul now tells how Christians are to act. These actions can only be accomplished with the help of the indwelling Holy Spirit. Knowing the battle between our flesh and spirit, Christians should feel no obligation to their flesh but rather one to the Lord, who now dwells by His Spirit within. The flesh is the source of the sinful desires that Christians battle against (Romans 7:5). Paul earlier stated that Christians were once slaves to sin (Romans 7:14) but are now slaves to righteousness (Romans 6:19). Paul further states that Christians have an obligation to walk according to the Spirit (Romans 8:4). Take a moment and think about that statement.

Paul says we are under an obligation to obey God, which is described as putting to death the deeds of the flesh. Thus, we are to live with our flesh in subjection to our spirit. This is accomplished by dying daily to the desires of the flesh (Romans 6:11), by considering it as dead (Colossians 3:5). God has empowered us to do so through the circumcision of the heart performed by the Holy Spirit (Colossians 2:11–13) and through His indwelling (sealing) presence (Ephesians 1:13–14). Think about what Jesus has done for you. We deserved nothing but His wrath, but have instead received blessings. I will be eternally grateful for what God has done for me, and I want to glorify Him with my remaining time on this earth.

Does the truth of His grace make you want to obey and serve Him more? Rather than encouraging license, God's amazing grace should encourage all Christians to pursue their sanctification (1 Timothy 6:11; 2 Timothy 2:22), including heeding when the grace of God instructs us to deny worldly desires (Titus 2:11–12). I know that I owe Jesus my life, and it frightens me to think where I would be without His grace and mercy.

Know that sin in a believer can lead to destruction. These ramifications can include things like lack of spiritual discernment (1 Corinthians 3:1–3) and sickness (Psalm 32:3–4, 38:3). Paul tells how Christians who continually follow after the desires of their flesh can face death as the consequence (Proverbs 11:19; 1 John 5:16). The importance of obedience in a Christian cannot be stressed enough.

◆ ◆ ◆

Verses 14–18

Christians, the sons and daughters of God.

6) Read Romans 8:14–16

a) Verse 14: What does the indwelling Holy Spirit do to Christians?

b) Verse 14: What title does He allow Christians to have?

c) Verse 15: What important fact does Paul remind the Christians of?

d) Verse 16: What does the Holy Spirit remind Christians of?

While Paul instructs us to reckon ourselves as dead and yield to the Spirit (Romans 6:11), he also tells how only Christians will be led to do so. The key is the indwelling Spirit who leads and causes believers to obey Him (Ezekiel 36:27). We were given a glimpse of this leading when the Holy Spirit was put amid the Jews during their time in the wilderness (Isaiah 63:11). When He lifted out the column of fire or cloud (Numbers 9:17–19), the Jews followed. When the Spirit stayed, the Jews remained camped. Christians have the advantage of the same Spirit living in them and should daily submit to His leading.

The presence of the Holy Spirit within a believer makes a huge difference in their life. This truth was previously unknown (Colossians 1:26–27) but is now revealed in the gospel. It would have been unfathomable for an Old Testament Jew to think that the God who is a consuming fire could live in someone without consuming them (Deuteronomy 4:24; Isaiah 33:14).

The indwelling Spirit leads and changes all Christians (1 John 3:24):

- He leads us first of all to Jesus (Psalm 61:2).

- He leads us in His will (Psalm 143:10).

- He teaches us in truth (John 14:23), using His Word (Psalm 43:3, Psalm 25:5).

- He leads us in His way (Psalm 27:11), which is the way we should go (Isaiah 48:17).

- He leads us to repentance (Romans 2:4), in His righteousness (Psalm 5:8).

- He leads us to rest (Ezekiel 34:15).

We should daily submit to the will of God and request His leading (Psalm 31:3, 43:3, 143:10). This will propel our sanctification forward (2 Thessalonians 2:13). Recognize that spending time in the Word of God is also a key to living an obedient life (John 17:17). Those who the Holy Spirit leads are now free from God's Law (2 Corinthians 3:17; Galatians 5:18). This results in freedom from slavery to sin (Galatians 4:7), including freedom from the fear of death, and punishment (Hebrews 2:15; 1 John 4:18). This new relationship to sin is one of the proofs of salvation.

The knowledge of our right standing with God results in the absence of fear, which encourages Christians to confidently come into the presence of their loving Abba Father (Ephesians 3:12; Galatians 4:6). Jesus also called His Father the same name (Mark 14:36). This helps to explain how Jesus calls Christians both His children and brethren (Hebrews 2:11–13; Isaiah 8:17–18). The indwelling Holy Spirit reveals to Christians their true identity, bearing witness that they are part of the family of God (Ephesians

1:5).

Christians know they are in the family of God because the Holy Spirit tells them so! This truth alone should inspire Christians not to use their freedom as an opportunity to indulge in the desires of the flesh (Galatians 5:13; 1 Peter 2:16). In verse 16, we are assured by God's Spirit and His Word that we are the sons of God. Only those who receive Christ are given the right to that title (John 1:12).

7) Read Romans 8:17–18

a) Verse 17: What can Christians look forward to?

b) Verse 18: What does Paul say about any sufferings we might endure?

c) Verse 18: What can't the sufferings of this world be compared to?

Just as earthly children are heirs of their earthly fathers, only Christians are heirs of the kingdom of God (Acts 20:32; Titus 3:7). Know that this blessing is only available by faith (Hebrews 9:15, 11:7–9), and should encourage Christians to endure until the end (Hebrews 6:11). While He is an eternal part of the Trinity, we are also told that God's only Son, Jesus Christ is also called an heir (Hebrews 1:2). Unlike the inheritance that is by grace that Christians receive, the inheritance that Jesus receives is His divine right (Philippians 2:6; 2 Corinthians 2:9). His action on the cross on our behalf made us heirs with Him.

We are told that Christians will experience suffering while on this earth. This is proof of their salvation (1 Peter 4:14). Trials reveal the true identity of self-proclaimed Christians, as many will shrink back and abandon the faith when faced with persecution. Jesus warned how His followers would be persecuted and hated (Luke 6:22; Matthew 5:10–12; John 15:18-20). This truth is much different from the false gospel of prosperity that many Christians are given. The result is a group of people who are not prepared for the suffering that God plainly states that all true Christians will face (2 Corinthians 1:5; Colossians 1:24; 1 Peter 4:13).

The good news is that our future glorification with Jesus is secure (Colossians 3:4). Jesus alone is the author of salvation (Hebrews 2:10), who will bring Christians to the glory (1 John 3:2) that will not be revealed until the rapture (John 5:28–29; 1 Corinthians 15:41–52). This is when all Christians will receive their resurrected bodies (1 Corinthians 15:22–23, 44–49; Philippians 3:20–21). Only at that time will believers be completely delivered from sin forever.

How can we apply these important truths when suffering for the faith? By keeping "this present time" in the proper perspective (2 Corinthians 4:17). God says to rejoice; you are a child of God, and your name is written in the Book of Life (Luke 10:20; 1 John 3:1). The fact that we have a secure future in Heaven with our Father should be a great comfort in any trial. When God tells us to seek wisdom (James 1:5), He means seeing things through the eyes of God in the context of eternity. The world sees things from this side of eternity, which is just the opposite of God's view. Remember, God's perspective is eternal. Our time on this earth and the sufferings we endure for the sake of the gospel are insignificant when compared to the eternity we will have in glory.

Verses 19–23

God's eternal plan was for all of creation to be free from sin.

8) Read Romans 8:19–22

a) Verse 19: What is creation eagerly waiting for?

b) Verse 20: What was creation subjected to?

c) Verse 20: Who did the subjecting?

d) Verse 20: Why?

e) Verse 21: What is God's eternal purpose?

f) Verse 22: What is creation described as having?

While one might think they know who the children of God are (Matthew 7:21–23; Revelation 21:7), we won't know for sure until they are revealed when Jesus returns (Philippians 3:20). This will be a great day for not only His children but also the rest of Creation which was called good before the original sin (Genesis 1:31) and the curse that caused it to also suffer from slavery to corruption (Genesis 3:17–19, 5:29).

God knew that sin had to be defeated in order to have a perfect creation. When God laid the foundation of the earth (Hebrews 1:10), He already had an eternal plan for a perfect creation (Daniel 9:24). He allowed Adam and Eve to sin, knowing that the temporary effects would be overshadowed by the result (through Jesus) which would be a perfect creation where sin would have already been defeated. Jesus spoke of this time when teaching His disciples concerning their future reward (Matthew 19:27–28).

Besides Christians, all of Creation will also be freed from the effects it suffers due to sin. We are given a glimpse of the future by the prophet Isaiah, telling how the animals will be at peace with each other during the millennial rule of Christ (Isaiah 11:6–9). Just as a mother's pain in childbirth was part of the curse, Creation suffers similar pains. This is confirmed by the fact that Creation is decaying. Like the joy experienced at the birth of a child, a time when the pain is forgotten, Creation itself will rejoice at the conclusion of its suffering (2 Corinthians 4:16–18). This will be a new and perfect Creation designed for eternity called the new heaven and new earth (2 Peter 3:13; Revelation 21:1).

There is no part of Creation untouched by sin. Sin is why there is sickness. Sin is the problem behind pain, death, and sorrow. Sin is why there is hell. Sin is why there are earthquakes and hurricanes. Sin is why there are weeds. Sin is why there is drought and famine. Sin is probably why there are mosquitoes and is definitely why there are cats (just kidding).

❖ ❖ ❖

Verses 23–27

The blessings of having the indwelling Holy Spirit.

9) Read Romans 8:23–25

a) Verse 23: Whom have Christians been given?

b) Verse 23: What are Christians waiting for?

c) Verse 24: How are Christians saved?

d) Verse 25: What do we hope for?

e) Verse 25: What character trait does a Christian now have?

At conversion, Christians are given the right to be called a child of God (John 1:12) because they are now legally adopted into His family. As a direct result, they now have the Holy Spirit within them as a first fruit (Romans 8:15) and a pledge for their future inheritance (2 Corinthians 1:22). Paul describes their remaining time on this earth as living in an earthly tent and groaning for a future time when they will receive their resurrected body (2 Corinthians 5:1–5).

Why does our spirit groan? Because we want to be set free from the weaknesses and desires of the flesh that we still live in. Jesus might have been alluding to our new bodies when He told of our mansions in Heaven (John 14:2–3).

The proof of the indwelling Spirit is the fruits a Christian exhibits (Galatians 5:22–23). These fruits give hope for our future guaranteed redemption, which is the consummation of our adoption (1 Thessalonians 5:8; Ephesians 1:13–14). We are eagerly awaiting our glorification, which is the final step of our redemption (1 Peter 1:13). This will happen when the rapture occurs, a time when every believer will be transformed and conformed to the body of Christ's glory (Philippians 3:20–21; Colossians 3:4).

Paul reminds us that it was our faith in the gospel that saved us, and it is our faith in what we don't yet see that sustains us (2 Corinthians 5:7; Hebrews 11:1). Until that time, we are to endure (Hebrews 10:36) by putting on the helmet of salvation (Ephesians 6:17; 1 Thessalonians 5:8). That said, only true Christians will endure until the end (Hebrews 3:14), which will be a time when the temporal will be replaced by the eternal (2 Corinthians 4:16–18). Christians persevere, knowing that the God of the Bible, who cannot lie (Titus 1:2; Hebrews 6:18), declares that their salvation is protected by the power of God (1 Peter 1:5).

10) Read Romans 8:26–27

a) Verse 26: How does the Holy Spirit help believers?

b) Verse 26: What do believers not always know?

c) Verse 27: What advantage does the Holy Spirit have?

Besides our sure hope, how does the indwelling Holy Spirit play a huge part in a believer's endurance and perseverance? By interceding for Christians (Hebrews 7:25) and helping them in their weaknesses, including the challenge of responding to God's invitation to pray. This is important because we don't always know how or what to pray. Christians have the blessing of the Holy Spirit praying for God's will in our lives.

God is clear that Christians only see dimly (1 Corinthians 13:9–12). Because of this, we don't always know God's will (1 John 5:14). This is why Jesus instructed and demonstrated to us how to pray for God's will in our lives (Matthew 6:10). One major purpose for our prayers should always be to seek and ask for God's will in our lives. Jesus modeled this in His own prayer life (Luke 22:42). Our prayers should be filtered through what the Word of God reveals as His will for our lives. When praying for something not necessarily revealed in Scripture, I believe it is best to include the qualification of "no matter what, let Your will be done."

We can trust the will of God, as He knows the beginning from the end (Proverbs 20:24; Isaiah 46:10). More importantly, we can trust He has a will, and it is always for His glory and our welfare (Jeremiah 29:11). The Holy Spirit's intercession is perfect because He searches our hearts and prays for our needs according to God's will. Remember that when the Holy Spirit prays, it is always according to the will of the Father! Christians should be comforted knowing that God is active in their lives, as He not only hears but answers their prayers (Matthew 7:9).

◆ ◆ ◆

Verses 28–30

Paul describes some of God's will for our lives and how He accomplishes it.

11) Read Romans 8:28–30

a) Verse 28: What do we know about God?

b) Verse 28: Whom does He do this for?

c) Verse 28: What are Christians called for?

d) Verse 29: What is God's purpose?

e) Verse 30: How is the process defined?

God is sovereign and always in control. He has an eternal plan (Ephesians 3:11) and makes sure it is accomplished (Ephesians 1:11). This includes times when God permits adversity in our lives. This was exemplified by King Asa, who, when faced with Baasha, the King of Israel, coming against him, bribed Ben-Hadad (King of Syria) to come to his aid rather than seek the counsel of the Lord. Asa tried to solve the problem with his wisdom and strength because he did not realize that the Lord was giving him an opportunity to defeat both Baasha and Ben-Hadad and have many years of peace (2 Chronicles 16). And he never stopped to ask God's guidance.

Just like Asa, there are many times that Christians fail to wait on God and seek to solve problems with their strength and wisdom. When faced with a trial, we are not to rush into judgment but rather seek the Lord and His will (James 1:5). Notice how God states that His will is for the good of those who love Him. This means that God can and will make something good come out of terrible things that come into our lives.

Does this mean He causes the terrible things that come into our lives? No, but He allows them to happen. We live in a fallen world where tragedy simply happens as a result of the Fall. God tells us that His will for our lives is from eternity. Christians have been predestined not only to be God's children (1 John 3:1; Ephesians 1:3–4) but also to be conformed to the image of Jesus Christ (1 Peter 1:2).

Does this mean that God predestines only those who would choose Him? No! There is nothing in Scripture that supports a doctrine that God reacts to events. If true, it would mean that God does not know the future. God is, in fact, proactive rather than reactive. Just as the death and resurrection of Jesus was God's eternal plan (Acts 2:23; 1 Corinthians 2:7), so was a people being prepared for His own possession (Titus 2:14; 1 Peter 2:9).

This means that the good which God causes is our sanctification, which glorifies Him and prepares us for eternity (2 Thessalonians 2:13–14). Just as Adam was the firstborn of those in the flesh (1 Corinthians 15:45), Jesus is the firstborn or preeminent head of those born in the Spirit (Colossians 1:15–18). The result is that those in Adam are dead, while those in Christ are alive (1 Corinthians 15:22).

We are shown the sequence of God's calling:

- He has known His children for all eternity.

- He predestines and then calls those whom He chose (2 Timothy 1:9).

- The next step for the called individual is to exercise their gift of faith, resulting in justification (Ephesians 2:8).

- Those justified are then glorified.

All of these are solely accomplished by God. Notice how Paul uses the past tense when discussing the future glorification of Christians (Romans 8:30). This is to show how their future glorification is a sure thing! Jesus has brought the chance for salvation to everyone, as all sins were placed upon Him while on the cross (Isaiah 53:6). While God does predestine some, He calls everyone to Himself (Matthew 11:28), and His desire is that none should perish (2 Peter 3:9). While everyone is called (Matthew 22:14), only those chosen will respond to the call of the gospel (John 8:37, 47). The next steps for those responding to the call are justification (1 Corinthians 6:11), sanctification (Titus 2:14), and then glorification (John 17:22).

Verses 31–39

God's promise of eternal security.

12) Read Romans 8:31–34

a) Verse 31: Who is for Christians?

b) Verse 32: What enables God to be for us?

c) Verse 32: What does He give us?

d) Verse 33: Does God accuse Christians?

e) Verse 33: What is God's response to accusations?

f) Verse 34: Does God condemn Christians?

g) Verse 34: Who intercedes?

Paul has just told how Christians have been predestined; He now stresses how the result is that God is for us. Paul asks seven questions to remove any doubt concerning where Christians stand with the Almighty God. Make no mistake about this truth.

God is for Christians (Psalm 118:6). Satan is the accuser of the brethren (Revelation 12:10). God is the ultimate judge, and only His opinion matters. While Satan wants us to believe otherwise, who can undo God's declaration that Christians are righteous?

How do we know for sure that God is for those He predestined? Because of the gift of His only Son, Jesus Christ, whom He delivered to death for our sins! The Father's plan for our security included ensuring that our debt was paid in full by sending His only Son to pay it Himself (Colossians 2:14; John 3:16). Paul earlier stated that Christians are not condemned for their sins (Romans 8:1).

How can God bring a charge against Christians (Isaiah 50:8) when He Himself declares them as righteous (1 Corinthians 6:11)? Jesus Himself defends Christians by using the precious blood He has shed (Revelation 12:11), His blood which cleanses believers from all their sin (1 John 1:7). God's Word is clear; all sin was dealt with by Jesus on the cross. Scripture is also clear that God will judge the world through Jesus Christ, whom He has raised from the dead (Acts 17:31).

Paul tells how He will not condemn the elect He has chosen and shed His blood for. Paul reminds us that Jesus cannot condemn, as He has died for our sins (Romans 5:6), been raised for our life (Romans 4:25), and is now at the right hand of the Father interceding for us (Mark 16:19; Hebrews 7:25). These truths are so important because Satan uses religion to paint a different picture than this Biblical reality. Realize that God does not condemn but rather defends Christians. Think about the basics of a court of law. There is the judge, someone prosecuting, and someone defending. The Father is the judge, Jesus is the defender, and Satan is the accuser.

How can Christians be condemned when God Himself is defending us? The answer is they can't because Jesus died and was resurrected from the dead! The accuser no longer has a case—he has been defeated.

13) Read Romans 8:35–39

a) Verse 35: What question does Paul ask?

b) Verse 38 & 39: What is Paul's answer?

c) Verse 35: What things can we expect to happen to us?

d) Verse 36: What truth does Paul remind us of?

e) Verse 37: What is the result of our tribulation?

f) Verses 38 & 39: Is there anything that can separate us from the love of God?

No created thing can separate a Christian from God's love! This chapter, which began with no condemnation (Romans 8:1), now ends with no separation (Romans 8:39–40). Earlier, Paul told us that Christians would suffer for their faith (Romans 8:17–18); he now tells us that trials and tribulations cannot separate us from God's love.

While many who experience trials will naturally feel that God has withdrawn His love, nothing is farther from the truth. While on this earth, Christians will have to endure trials (Philippians 1:29; John 16:33). This truth is very different from what the prosperity gospel promises. While at times it may appear that the world is victorious, the reality is that Christians (through Jesus) are the conquerors (1 Corinthians 15:54–57). It should be considered an honor to suffer for the name of Jesus (Acts 5:41; 1 Peter 3:17).

The good news is we will not and cannot be separated from the love that God has for us (2 Timothy 1:12). Paul knew and experienced this truth very well (2 Corinthians 4:11, 11:26). Paul reminds us that tribulation should not come as a surprise because God's Word foretold it would happen (Psalm 44:22). Despite these things Christians have a sure victory (1 John 5:4).

◆ ◆ ◆

This closes what might be the most important chapter in the entire Bible. Again, it started with no condemnation and ended with no separation. Know this benefit is for Christians only. While hard to understand during life's difficult trials, we can trust that God is for us! The blessed reality of God's unbreakable love is something that Christians should daily remind themselves of having received.

CHAPTER NINE

What about the chosen Jews?

◆ ◆ ◆

Verses 1–13

Paul deals with a hypothetical question.
What about the Jews? How can Christians be sure of their election,
knowing that the chosen Jews are not saved?

1) Read Romans 9:1–5

a) Verses 1-3: Describe Paul's feelings toward the Jews.

b) Verse 3: How does Paul describe his relationship with them?

c) Verses 4 & 5: What benefits did the Israelites have

d) Verse 5: What nation was Messiah born into?

e) Verse 5: How is Jesus described?

Paul goes to the extent of claiming both Jesus and the Holy Spirit as witnesses for his great sorrow and grief over his lost countrymen. While he might have looked like he was against the Jews as he left Judaism, and his gospel had the appearance of being against the Law, nothing was farther from the truth (Acts 18:13, 21:28). Paul greatly suffered at the hands of his countryman (Acts 22:22). For instance, by the time this epistle was (58 AD), written, he had been given thirty-nine lashes five times by the Jews (2 Corinthians 11:24). Due to Jewish opposition, Paul was beaten by Roman magistrates at Philippi (Acts 16:23). Jews came from Antioch and Iconium and incited the crowds at Lystra to stone Paul and leave him for dead (Acts 14:19). All this, yet he still loved his kinsmen.

Paul was reflecting the heart of God, who grieves over those who reject Him. This was exemplified by Jesus grieving over the Jews who failed to recognize He was fulfilling Daniel's prophecy concerning His revelation as the Messiah (Luke 19:41–44; Daniel 9:25). Jesus also wept over Jerusalem, telling how His desire was for the salvation of the people there (Luke 13:34). Notice how Paul states that he could (not would) wish himself accursed for the salvation of the Jews who are not chosen (Exodus 32:31–32). But would this make a difference?

Can we do something for someone else's salvation? How about praying for them? How about baptizing an infant? God's clear answer is no one is born again either by the will of the flesh or the will of man (John 1:13).

How can we apply this truth? By understanding that we cannot do anything for the unsaved except deliver the gospel in love (Romans 1:16). Salvation is an individual decision, and no one can decide for anyone else to follow Jesus.

Notice how Paul first acknowledged how the Jews were related to him only in flesh (Romans 1:3). The true spiritual brothers and sisters in the Lord are Christians (Matthew 12:50). While the Jews had great advantages, Paul (a Jew himself) knew that Jesus had brought and ordained the New Covenant (Jeremiah 31:31–34), which is far superior to the Law (Hebrews 8:6). God's Word tells us there is something more important than being a blood descendant of Abraham (Matthew 3:9; Luke 3:8).

Paul tells how the descendants of Jacob (Genesis 35:10; Isaiah 41:8-9; Psalm 147:19–20) were recipients of God's promises to Abraham (Genesis 12, 15, 17, 22). The Israelites were adopted as sons (Exodus 4:22), blessed with seeing the Shekinah glory of God (Exodus 40:34), and were given both the Law and the Temple (Deuteronomy 4:13). The covenants, the Law, temple service and the promises of God to Israel all pointed to Messiah. Besides the great patriarchs, the Messiah came through the nation of Israel, just as promised (Genesis 49:10; Isaiah 11:10). Also, just as promised, the Messiah is not only God for the Jews (Isaiah 9:6) but the blessed God over all (Romans 1:25; Psalm 72:18). By stating this, Paul is confirming that Jesus is God (Colossians 1:16–19; Titus 2:13).

2) Read Romans 9:6–7

a) Verse 6: Has the Word of God failed?

b) Verses 6 & 7: Why not?

c) Verse 7: Who are Abraham's chosen descendants?

Paul now begins to expound on what he declared in Romans 9:3, first stating that the Word of God has not failed. How can he say that? Because it does not make progress in those not predestined (John 8:37–39, 43). Paul then makes a profound claim and seems to confirm it with a contradictory statement. He first makes the incredible declaration that not all of Israel is descended from Israel. Paul then reminds us how the Lord told Abraham that even though Ishmael was his descendant (Genesis 17:19, 21:12), God's choice was Isaac.

What does this mean? Are not all the Jews descendants of Isaac and his son Jacob? Can't all Jews count on their lineage to Abraham (John 8:39)? How, then, are they not all Israel? Paul alluded to this truth when he earlier told how the true Jews are not those simply circumcised in the flesh (Romans 2:28–29), but those who have the circumcision of the heart (Jeremiah 9:25). To better understand this, one needs to look into Paul's letter to the Galatians, as it gives further insight into what God is stating here. In this letter, he describes two different types of people.

He first states how Abraham had two sons (Galatians 4:22). Ishmael, the child of the bondwoman (Hagar, Genesis 16:15), is described as a child of the flesh (Galatians 4:23). Isaac, the child of the free woman (Sarah, Genesis 18:10, 21:2), is described as the child of the promise (Galatians 4:23; Hebrews 11:11) who was born according to the spirit (Galatians 4:28).

The two children are an analogy of two different types of people (Galatians 4:24). The first group is (just like Isaac) called the children of the promise, who are representative of the chosen Christians (Galatians 4:28, 31). The second group is (just like Ishmael) called the children of the flesh (not predestined) (Galatians 4:23). Paul also wrote that Ishmael persecuted Isaac just as Christians even today are persecuted by non-Christians (Galatians 4:29). He also told how Christians are children of the free woman (Galatians 4:31). Keep these truths in mind as we continue discussing this chapter.

3) Read Romans 9:8

a) Exactly who are the children of God?

b) Who are not the children of God?

Paul can state that the Word of God has not failed because he knew that not all of Israel is spiritual Israel. He also knew that being chosen had nothing to do with being a Jew (John 8:37). Make no mistake about this. The spiritually chosen people are Christians, and this choice transcends race (Revelation 5:9). Let me repeat this important truth. The spiritually chosen people are Christians. You might ask whether this means that God has turned His back on the Jews. Absolutely not! Paul will confirm this fact in Chapter Eleven.

As we just discussed, the children of the promise are also the children of God (Galatians 4:22–31; Matthew 13:38), who are the seed of Abraham (Galatians 3:16, 29). Even though they might even be Jewish, the children of the flesh are not considered the true children of Abraham (Galatians 4:23). Paul earlier described how God predestined Christians (Romans 8:29–30). This Scripture gives better insight into the sovereignty of God. Christians are the children of the promise! That is, it is not the children of the flesh who are children of God, but the children of the promise are regarded as descendants.

4) Read Romans 9:9–13

a) Verse 9: What promise to Abraham does God refer to?

b) Verse 10: What are we told about Isaac's wife Rebecca?

c) Verse 12 & 13: What did the Lord state concerning her twins?

d) Verse 11: Was this before she had given birth?

e) Verse 11: Was God's choice of Jacob based on works?

f) Verse 11: Why not?

The God of the Bible reveals His sovereignty in these verses. We are told the Lord informed Abraham that within a year (Genesis 17:19, 18:10), his ninety-year-old wife Sarah would have a son (Isaac). It was by faith that Isaac was conceived (Hebrews 11:11); thus, he was a child of the promise. God chose Isaac to be the symbolic spiritual father of a specific people and also the literal father of a specific people who would bring forth the promised Messiah.

Later, Isaac was forty years old when he married Rebekah (Genesis 25:20). After being barren for almost twenty years, Rebekah conceived twins and was told by the Lord that she had two nations in her womb (Genesis 25:23). Just as God chose Isaac over Ishmael (Genesis 17:21, 21:12), He rejected the firstborn twin Esau and chose Jacob as the one through whom the promises would come (Genesis 35:10–12; Malachi 1:2–3). God's choice was not influenced by any works or faith and was made before the twins had even been born. This shows how God's election is not based on anything but His sovereign choice.

Isn't this unfair? God is always just and can do with His creation whatever He desires (Exodus 33:19). His choices happen from all eternity (Ephesians 1:4; 2 Thessalonians 2:13).

Does God have the right to determine who He will spend eternity with? It is important to remember that Jesus desires that everyone be saved (1 Timothy 2:4). He died for everyone (Titus 2:11), taking all their sins upon Himself on the cross (Isaiah 53:6). He is patient with the children of the flesh. He loves and blesses them (John 3:16), inviting them into a relationship with Him (Matthew 11:28; John 7:37). He promises salvation to all who call on Him (John 1:21; Acts 2:21). Despite all this, the children of the flesh still reject Him (John 5:39–40).

Is God to blame for people rejecting Him? Notice how we are told that God hated Esau. Does this mean that God hates? No, God is love, and this fact was exhibited on the cross (1 John 4:8). But did God "hate" Esau? No, it means He chose to bestow on Jacob and not Esau the blessings of the covenant He made to Abraham. While this is described as hate, it is better defined as "loved or blessed less." Examples of this are given in both the Old (Genesis 29:31; Deuteronomy 21:15) and New Testaments (Matthew 6:24; Luke 14:26; John 12:25). Know that God chose to bless Esau with both possessions and descendants (Genesis 33:8, 36).

Verses 14–20

Paul reminds us of the sovereignty of God.

5) Read Romans 9:14–16

a) Verse 14: Is God unjust?

b) Verse 15: In declaring His sovereignty, what two terms are used by God?

c) Verse 16: What are we told about God?

d) Verse 16: Do works factor in God's sovereignty?

Paul now deals with any questions concerning the perceived unfairness one might question concerning predestination. Remember, through Jesus, God has shed His grace on everyone. Paul reminds us that God is just (Zechariah 9:9). God is not only perfect (Matthew 5:48; Hebrews 5:9), He is also impartial (2 Chronicles 19:7; Romans 2:11).

It is imperative to realize that while God is not fair, He is always just, and there is a big difference between the two. The parable of the landowner illustrates this point (Matthew 20:1–15). The landowner is accused of being unfair for giving the same wage to the individuals who worked one hour as those who worked all day. This was even though those who worked all day had agreed on their pay. Let me point out that while the landowner could be called unfair, he could not be called unjust, as those who worked all day received their agreed-upon wage. This has no bearing on the fact that the landowner decided to be merciful with those who had only worked an hour. The truth is God owns everything, and He can do what He pleases (Matthew 20:15).

God answers to no one. Notice how God uses the words "mercy" and "compassion" when declaring His sovereignty (Exodus 33:19). It is important to realize this conversation between God and Moses occurred after the Jews had made and worshipped a golden calf (Exodus 32:4–6). The Lord could have destroyed the entire nation, but He chose to be merciful with only three thousand falling (Exodus 32:28). The fact is that God's mercy and compassion are also part of the "unfairness" He practices with us! Notice how we are told that God's mercy does not depend on the man who wills but rather on Him alone! This confirms Paul's earlier statement (Romans 9:11). This is why Gentiles are saved (Isaiah 65:1). Even in His sovereignty, God is merciful. Realize that mercy means not getting what is deserved.

Take a deep breath and think about that statement then ask yourself these questions:

- *What do I deserve from God?*

- *Does God owe me anything?*

- *Have I ever been faithful to Him?*

- *Did God choose me because I was better than anyone else?*

- *Am I also guilty like the rest of the world (Romans 3:10, 23)?*

- *Do I not deserve God's wrath?*

When questioning God's love for humanity or whether God is just, one must keep in mind that the Father mercifully sent His only Son to pay the price of death for everyone (John 3:16; Titus 2:11, 3:4). This includes those who not only reject Him but also persecute His children.

6) Read Romans 9:17-18

a) Verse 17: Why did God create and raise Pharaoh?

b) Verse 18: What does God do?

While Moses was shown mercy, Pharaoh was also created for God's glory (Exodus 9:16). Know that all creation is made for the glory of the God of the Bible, who wants His power and name to be known throughout the earth. God used the circumstances of the Exodus for this to be accomplished. Even though Pharaoh had already witnessed multiple plagues, he still rejected God, who could have justly killed him, but rather let him remain so His power would be proclaimed throughout the earth. Is this not a perfect illustration of God's mercy that Paul just wrote of?

We are shown how this purpose was fulfilled three hundred years later when the Philistines referred to what God had done for the Jews (1 Samuel 4:8). Even today, the example of the Exodus is still used as a witness to the power and faithfulness of the God of the Bible (Exodus 15:11). While God did harden Pharaoh (Exodus 4:21, 7:3, 10:20, 10:27, 11:10, 14:4), it was the sin in his life that allowed it his heart to be hardened. Pharaoh resisted the Lord, and the result was hardening his own heart (Exodus 8:15, 19).

This is just as Paul describes what will happen as a result of rejecting the one true God (Romans 1:24–25; Psalm 81:11–12). God was not at fault for Pharaoh rejecting Him, as He only uses what is already present within an individual (Hebrews 3:8). Because salvation is so simple, everyone who rejects Jesus will have brought on their judgment (Jeremiah 2:17, 19, 4:18; John 3:18). Conversely, everyone who comes to Jesus will have been drawn by the Father (Luke 10:21; John 6:44). The Old Testament reveals how the sovereign God's purpose was also fulfilled by hardening the kings of the north to go into battle against the Jews (Joshua 11:20).

Balance the truth that God can do with His creation what He pleases (Job 12:23; Acts 17:26) with the fact that He takes no pleasure in the death of the wicked (Ezekiel 33:11). The real fact is that the God of the Bible is just, whether or not He is merciful toward any of us who deserve nothing but His wrath. God has promised that the wages of sin is death (Romans 6:23). He has also promised that those who put their trust in Jesus will be saved (Acts 2:21). Are these two choices not simple? Again, do not confuse the difference between fair and just.

6) Read Romans 9:19–20

a) Verse 19: What is a possible response to God's sovereignty?

b) Verse 20: What is God's answer?

One typical response to the revelation of God's sovereignty might be to question why He finds fault in those who reject Him. Who can resist His will? Let us stop right here and get this straight. God's desire is not for anyone to perish (2 Peter 3:9). His sovereignty does not release man from his responsibility for his actions. God promises salvation to everyone who places their trust in Jesus (John 1:12, 3:16). Don't blame God for the fact that people reject Him. This ridiculous argument is not much different from the possible response Paul dealt with concerning man's unrighteousness demonstrating the righteousness of God (Romans 3:5–7).

Think about this question for a moment. Can God be blamed for sin? Isn't it so typical of a man not to take responsibility for his actions? One of the principal characteristics of our fallen nature is our habit of assigning blame to others (including God) for wrong choices we have made (Genesis 3:12, 13). Paul refers to this argument as talking back to God. Do you think anyone will be talking back to God at the White Throne Judgment (Revelation 20:11–13)? Do you think that sinful mankind will judge the perfect God (Genesis 18:25; Deuteronomy 32:4)?

Ask yourself these questions:

- *Does God have an eternal plan for Creation?*

- *Is God holy and just?*

- *Has He not shed His grace on all of mankind (Titus 2:11)?*

- *Did He not die for everyone's sin (Isaiah 53:6)?*

Now, balance your answers with the following questions:

• Did God cause people to turn away from Him to idols (Isaiah 65:2)?

• Did not the Jews turn from the Lord despite all the blessings they received and miracles they witnessed?

• Did Jesus cause Judas to betray Him? Was it God's mercy that caused these sins?

• Could a just God judge sinners if they had no choice?

• Does anyone even have the right to question the motives or actions of a perfect God?

Isaiah tells how man has turned things around (Isaiah 29:16), somehow believing that the clay is equal to the potter (Jeremiah 18:3–6). Isaiah also reminds us that the clay has no right to complain about the potter (Isaiah 45:9).

❖ ❖ ❖

Verses 21–29

God's purpose for Creation.

7) Read Romans 9:21–24

    a) Verse 21: How is God described?

    b) Verse 21: What can He do with the clay?

    c) Verse 21: Does God have the right to make different types of vessels?

    d) Verses 21 & 22: What types of vessels are described?

    e) Verses 22 & 23: What trait of God is revealed in the way He endures vessels of wrath?

    f) Verses 23 & 24: Who notices this?

Know that God is the potter (Isaiah 64:8), and we are the clay. No one has the right to question God or His motives because He has absolute right over His creation. Paul alludes to Jeremiah to make the point that God can do whatever He pleases and use whomever He pleases (Jeremiah 18:6). It is important to note that the context of Jeremiah 18 is God using Nebuchadnezzar as a vessel to pour out judgment on Judah (Jeremiah 25:7–9; 2 Kings 24:3). His message is He has dominion over the Jews and can use whomever He desires to bring judgment.

The prophet Habakkuk also questioned how God could use a wicked nation (Babylon) to bring judgment on Judah (Habakkuk 1:12–13). God answered by pointing out that the Jews were no more righteous than the Babylonians and that those who are righteous live by faith (Habakkuk 2:4). Paul applies this truth by using a rhetorical question to tell how there are common vessels (of wrath) and honorable vessels (of mercy). God decided to make Pharaoh (a common vessel) as well as make Moses and Aaron. People make themselves common vessels by refusing to honor God by exchanging the truth for a lie, ultimately worshipping something else (Romans 1:21–25).

No one can question the mercy and patience God has exhibited toward the vessels of wrath (2 Peter 3:9; 2 Thessalonians 1:9). He pleads to the unsaved that they repent and be saved (Acts 3:19–20, 26:20). They make themselves vessels of wrath by denying their Creator (Isaiah 59:13) and pursuing a life of sin (Romans 6:16).

What did we learn from the Exodus? While God was going to be faithful to His promise to Jacob (Genesis 35:11–12), He also chose to orchestrate the events of the Exodus in order for His Name to be made known to all the earth. The result was to His glory! The Jewish people had been greatly afflicted by the Egyptians (Exodus 3:7). There is no denying that God was patient with Pharaoh. He allowed him to remain, as His plan was to be glorified and reveal His power (Exodus 9:16).

Exactly who benefited from the events of the Exodus? The chosen nation of Israel, as God revealed His faithfulness to the promises He made to Abraham (Genesis 15:13–14; Exodus 3:8).

Was God was justified in killing the firstborn of Egypt (Exodus 12:29, 30)? Think about it as a just consequence for the Egyptians killing the sons of the Jews (Exodus 1:22; Acts 7:19).

Was it just for the Jews to leave with the possessions of the Egyptians (Exodus 13:35–36)? Think about it as a just delayed compensation for their many years of slavery (Genesis 15:14).

Christians (vessels of honor) could never fully understand God's mercy without a point of comparison. Paul understood the mercy of God very well (1 Timothy 1:13–16) because he had persecuted Christians and yet was still saved (Acts 8:1; 1 Corinthians 15:9). God's eternal plan is for Christians to forever rejoice in the gift of salvation they received (Psalm 13:5; Hebrews 8:12).

How could we ever fully appreciate the mercy we have been shown unless we witnessed the wrath of God (Proverbs 16:4)? God has a plan, and it is for the eternal benefit of all Creation. Christians have been given the gift of eternal life, even though we deserve nothing but God's wrath. The result will be eternal gratitude to Jesus.

8) Read Romans 9:24–29

a) Verse 24: What did God do to the vessels of mercy?

b) Verse 24: From what groups has God predestined a people for Himself?

c) Verses 25 & 26: How does Hosea confirm this?

d) Verses 27 & 28: How did Isaiah confirm this?

e) Verse 27: What does the Lord say about the Jews?

f) Verse 29: What did Israel deserve?

After earlier stating how God is just in showing mercy and compassion to whomever He chooses (Romans 9:14–15), Paul illustrates this truth by reminding us how God has also called certain Gentiles to be children of the promise (Romans 9:6–8). He earlier dealt with the fact that God also chose the Gentiles for salvation (Romans 1:13, 3:29). Many Jews would have thought just the opposite, considering Gentiles only as vessels of wrath.

While the Jewish people looked down on the Gentiles as having no hope, God's intention has always been for everyone to have the opportunity to have a relationship with Him. Notice how the vessels of mercy were called by God (1 Corinthians 1:24; 2 Timothy 1:9). None of us should be surprised at the Jews' rejection of Jesus because the Old Testament told us how it would happen (Isaiah 53:1).

Paul illustrates God's sovereignty by telling how He turned from the Jews to include the Gentiles, who are also predestined to be called children of God (Hosea 1:10, 2:23; Isaiah 63:16). This is quite a statement. Gentiles can also be called children of God. This is in addition to and not in place of the Jews. This fact should not come as a surprise because God told Abraham how through Jesus all the *'nations'* (Hebrew word *goy* meaning *'Gentiles'*) would be blessed (Genesis 12:3, 22:18). God also declared that His name would be great among the *goy* or *'nations'* (Malachi 1:11).

The Old Testament gives two clear examples of God's compassion toward the Gentiles:

- The first was during the time of Elijah when, even though there were many hungry widows in Israel (1 Kings 17:1), God chose one from the Gentile town of Zarephath. He used Elijah to first bless both her and her son with an inexhaustible supply of oil and flour and then to bring her son back to life after he had become sick and died. It is important to note that the first miracle of raising the dead happened to a Gentile!

- The second example is during the time of Elisha (2 Kings 5). While there were many lepers in Israel, God used Elisha to heal Naaman (the Syrian captain) of his leprosy by instructing him to wash in the Jordan River seven times.

Notice how both Isaiah (Isaiah 28:16) and Joel (Joel 2:32) did not qualify their prophecies by stating that only Jews who believe in the Messiah would be delivered and not disappointed. Multiple prophets told of a future time when the nations (Gentiles) would join themselves to the Lord (Zechariah 2:11; Isaiah 56:6; Micah 4:2). God even foretold how He would pour forth His Spirit on all of mankind (Joel 2:28).

Paul continues dealing with the question of the chosen Jews' rejection of the Messiah by reminding us of the prophecies that only a remnant of Jews will be saved. The context of what Paul quoted was Sennacherib's invasion of Judah and siege of Jerusalem (Isaiah 10:22–23). The Lord is telling how, even though He had determined that most of Judah would fall, some would be saved. Because of His promises, God has preserved Israel. We are told it was the mercy of God that prevented Israel from being completely judged like Sodom and Gomorrah (Isaiah 1:9).

The timing of Isaiah Chapter One is the reign of Judah's King Hezekiah. By this time, the northern Kingdom of Israel had fallen, along with many of the cities of Judah. The Lord is telling how He preserved them just as He protected Lot and his daughters from the wrath He sent on Sodom and Gomorrah (Genesis 19:29–30). This would also ensure His promise of the coming Messiah through the nation of Israel. Just as God was previously faithful to Israel to fulfill His promises, He will also be faithful to preserve a remnant, which is proof of His mercy toward Israel. God's Word also tells how the remnant will be saved by the Messiah (Isaiah 59:20). All of this shows both God's mercy and His sovereignty in ensuring His eternal plan.

◆ ◆ ◆

Verses 30–33

How the Gentiles attained righteousness and why the Jews failed.

9) Read Romans 9:30–33

a) Verse 30: Exactly how did the Gentiles attain righteousness?

b) Verses 31 & 32: What prevented Israel from attaining righteousness?

c) Verses 32 & 33: Whom did the Jews stumble over?

d) Verse 33: What is God's promise concerning the Messiah?

Paul concludes this chapter's argument concerning the Jews in whom the Word of God seemed to fail (Romans 9:6). He first tells how the Gentiles attained righteousness because they pursued it by faith (Romans 3:22, 5:18). He then tells how the non-believing Jews failed because they pursued salvation by works of the Law.

Isn't salvation by works exactly what religion teaches? Do all the works you can and hope they are good enough, and forget about the fact that God states they are like filthy rags (Isaiah 64:6). Religion tells you to trust in man rather than God (Jeremiah 17:5), who clearly warns how man's way can seem right, but ultimately end with a failure to reach eternal life (Proverbs 14:12). God implores those who seek righteousness to look at the example of Abraham (Isaiah 51:1–2).

What do we know about Abraham? His faith and not his works were counted as righteousness (Genesis 15:6; Galatians 3:6).

Can God be clearer? The gospel is very simple (2 Corinthians 11:3). Faith and not works is necessary for salvation (Luke 8:12; 1 Peter 1:9; Galatians 2:16; 2 Timothy 1:9). The Jews failed to realize that salvation comes through the crucified Son of God (1 Corinthians 1:22–23); thus they stumbled over the Messiah (Isaiah 8:13–15). One reason they rejected Him was that they failed to recognize all of the hundreds of Scriptures He fulfilled.

What are we told about the Messiah? God promises that everyone who places their trust in Him will never be disappointed (Isaiah 28:16). Know that this promise is for everyone. Again, don't blame God for those who reject Him. This is because He has brought salvation to all men (Titus 2:11).

How can we apply God's truth concerning predestination? We can realize we cannot persuade anyone to become a Christian (1 Corinthians 1:17) and never assume that the worst sinner we encounter is on the list of those not predestined. God has entrusted all Christians with the gospel (1 Thessalonians 2:4), which is what He uses to save (Romans 1:16).

CHAPTER TEN

Obtaining the righteousness of God is not difficult.

Verses 1–5

Being zealous for God without knowledge still results in eternal death.

1) Read Romans 10:1–3

a) Verse 1: What is Paul's desire and prayer for the nation of Israel?

b) Verse 2: How are they described?

c) Verse 2: What don't they have?

d) Verse 3: What don't they know about?

e) Verse 3: What does this cause them to do?

f) Verse 3: Whose righteousness are they rejecting?

g) Verse 3: What is necessary to be subject to?

Paul now expounds on what he just stated in the last chapter (Romans 9:30–33). It is amazing that Paul still had a heart toward the Jews who had persecuted him (Romans 9:2). He now warns how one can be zealous for God, yet without the knowledge only found in the gospel of Jesus Christ. That means someone can be sincere in his beliefs, but he is sincerely wrong. Even today, many sincere people zealously place their faith in religion rather than in Jesus Christ. Before his initial encounter with Christ

(Acts 9:1–6), Paul had been zealous for God but without knowledge (Acts 22:3; Galatians 1:14).

Where do you find the proper knowledge, and why don't people find it? People fail to find it because they seek knowledge through either man or their church (Jeremiah 17:5). They neglect God's Word, which alone gives the needed knowledge (Luke 11:52; 2 Timothy 3:15) that leads to salvation by faith in Jesus (1 Corinthians 1:21).

Realize that anyone preaching and believing in the authority of Scripture has the keys to the kingdom. Thus, among the keys given to Peter was the key of knowledge (Matthew 16:19), which is, in fact, given to not only Peter but all Christians (Luke 11:52).

What do those who lack knowledge not know? The fact that Jesus is the Messiah, and His righteousness is free and available to anyone who puts their faith in Him (Romans 5:15, 6:23).

Why do they not know it? Because it is revealed in the gospel of Jesus Christ that they reject (Romans 1:16–17).

Who encourages this? Satan does, using religious leaders disguised as angels of light (Matthew 23:13; 2 Corinthians 11:14).

Why don't those from the present-day church of Rome know this? Again, because it is revealed in the gospel of Jesus Christ that the Catholic Church rejects.

How do they reject it? By making the same mistake that the zealous Jews made. They either don't know or don't trust what God says about salvation and try to establish their own righteousness, totally disregarding the fact that perfection is needed and Jesus has done everything necessary for one's salvation (Isaiah 64:6).

Look at these references from the Catholic Catechism:

- Salvation is a combination of things like faith (183), baptism (1256-57), and obeying the Commandments (2068).

- Sacraments are necessary for salvation (1129, 980, 1129), which is not by faith alone (1815), but by good works, sacraments, and grace.

- Salvation is brought by Mary's intercession (969).

- Sanctifying grace is initially infused by baptism (1999) and then continues to be infused by sacraments (1127) and good works (2010, 2027).

- Grace is earned, lost, and only regained through the sacraments of the church (1129).

- Grace is completely lost by mortal sin (1033, 1855, 1874) but restored through penance (1446).

- Grace is infused by sacraments (1127-1129) and good works (2010, 2027).

- Grace can be increased with good works (1212, 1392, 2010, 2027).

- One cannot be sure of one's state of grace (2005), as one can only hope for the grace of final perseverance (2016).

Does this sound like the gospel of Jesus Christ? Notice what was stated by the Church of Rome at the Council of Trent. "Nobody knows with certainty of faith, which permits of no error, that he has achieved the grace of God. Whoever shall affirm that men are justified solely by the imputation of the righteousness of Christ....let him be accursed."

Do these statements not contradict what the entire Book of Romans teaches? I once encountered an individual who had a hard time with my teaching concerning Catholicism. He stated that he just wanted everyone to "hear the Catholic gospel." I then asked him if he died that day, would he go to Heaven? He responded with, "I hope so." I responded with, "That is not much of a gospel." He offered no response.

Know this: the Catholic gospel does not promise salvation. It is only a gospel of a "hope for salvation." It instructs to do many things (works) with only the dim hope of getting to Heaven, resulting in no assurance. But the gospel of Jesus Christ states that all who put their faith in Him will be saved (John 3:16). Notice how Paul talks about submitting to the righteousness of God. The Greek word for *'subject'* is *hupotasso*, which means *'to obey, be under obedience.'* Knowing the truth is not enough since there is a responsibility to personally submit to God's righteousness. The gospel states that one must obey it (2 Thessalonians 1:8) or suffer God's wrath (Romans 2:8; 1 Peter 4:17).

Why doesn't the gospel talk about obedience to the law? Because it is impossible! Paul will now begin to tell us how this is done, first telling of man's failed attempt at righteousness.

2) Read Romans 10:4–5

a) Verse 4: What good news are we told about the Law?

b) Verse 5: What bad news are we told about those who are under the Law?

Paul tells how the Law is not the answer. The Law ends for the believer. Jesus lived a sin-free life, thus fulfilling the goal of the Law (Hebrews 4:15), which was only a tutor set in place until Christ came so one could be justified by faith (Galatians 3:24–25). Paul is stating that Christ is the end of the Law for those who trust in Him. This is because they have died, and the Law no longer has jurisdiction over them (Romans 7:1–4).

Those who either reject Messiah or remain under God's Law fall short of the requirement of perfection (Matthew 5:48; Romans 9:32). The Law shuts every mouth by revealing what sin is (Romans

3:20). The Law condemns (Romans 4:15), brings death (Romans 7:10), and was never intended to bring eternal life (Galatians 2:21). The good news is that Christians and only Christians are free from the Law (Galatians 5:18). God plainly warns those who trust in the Law for their righteousness that they are on their own, cursed and guilty (Galatians 3:10; James 2:10).

Isn't this where most people are? They are on their own, trusting that their own righteousness will be enough for them to escape the fires of hell.

What don't they know or acknowledge? That the righteousness of God is available by faith, and their self-established righteousness is like a filthy rag (Isaiah 64:6).

Verses 6–13

Paul tells how obtaining the righteousness of God is not difficult.

3) Read Romans 10:6–9

a) Verses 6 & 7: What does the righteousness based on faith say not to do?

b) Verses 8 & 9: What does the righteousness by faith say?

c) Verse 8: Where is the Word of God?

d) Verse 8: Where is the righteousness revealed?

e) Verse 9: How do you receive Christ's righteousness?

Paul had just talked about those having a zeal for God without knowledge. He now goes into detail about what the unsaved do not know. Opposite to what the unsaved Jews would have thought and what the world and the Church at Rome teach, God now encourages anyone who thinks that salvation is difficult to obtain.

ROMANS 10:6–7 ARE SOME OF THE MOST IMPORTANT VERSES IN THE ENTIRE BIBLE!

Look at Romans 10:6–7 again. This is exactly what religion teaches: that salvation is difficult. These verses state that unbelief wants to undo what Jesus has already done, as if He never came to earth from Heaven, died, or was ever raised from the grave. Paul is telling how Jesus has already done everything needed for one's salvation. Many professed followers of Jesus submit to a different gospel that rejects

Christ's righteousness (Galatians 1:8–9). The devil will use religion to acknowledge Jesus, but essentially states that more has to be done. Nothing is further from the truth!

Paul quotes Moses, who declared that obeying God is not difficult (Deuteronomy 30:11–14). No, obeying God is impossible unless one is saved (Romans 8:7). The key to understanding the following verse is the words "the righteousness by faith speaks as follows" (Romans 10:6). That is what the gospel says. Salvation is not about works! It is not difficult! We do not have to bring Messiah from either Heaven or the abyss, as He has already done this. Take a moment and compare what Moses and Paul wrote. Look specifically at the terms I have highlighted:

> *For this commandment which I command you today is not too difficult for you, nor is it out of reach. "It is not in heaven, that you should say, 'Who will go up to heaven for us to get it for us and make us hear it, that we may observe it?'" — Deuteronomy 30:11–12*

Moses refers to the Word of God as a commandment and asks who will go to Heaven and get it. Paul interprets what Moses writes by substituting Christ for the word commandment.

> *But the righteousness based on faith speaks as follows: "DO NOT SAY IN YOUR HEART, 'WHO WILL ASCEND INTO HEAVEN?' (that is, to bring Christ down), or 'WHO WILL DESCEND INTO THE ABYSS?' (that is, to bring Christ up from the dead)." — Romans 10:6–7*

Inspired by the Holy Spirit, Paul makes this substitution because Jesus is the Word of God (John 1:1, 1:14). Paul is stating that those who have committed to Jesus Christ (who have the righteousness that speaks by faith) and only those, can obey God. This is due to the fact they are dead to the Law and sin's power (Romans 6:7, 7:6; John 8:36). Most people in this world are slaves to sin and cannot obey God (Romans 6:14). Through the finished work of Jesus, God's Law is no longer a burden to Christians who have been empowered to obey God (Acts 15:10; 1 Peter 1:2).

So, what does the gospel say? Do you want Christ's righteousness? Do you want salvation? It is not obtained by works, by going to mass, or by receiving the sacraments or confession of sins. It is found in God's Word, who is the Messiah! It is in the gospel message he is preaching (Romans 1:17).

What does the righteousness based on faith speak? It states that the needed righteousness is in your heart and then confessed by your mouth! Yes, it is in your mouth! Confess Jesus as Lord and believe that God raised Him from the dead, and you will receive it and be saved (Matthew 10:32; 1 John 4:15). People need to know that when they reject the gospel, they also reject God's righteousness, which is available at no cost to everyone. Isn't this simple?

Take a minute and answer these questions.

- *Do I have Christ's righteousness?*

- *Do I understand that it is free and simple to obtain?*

- *Am I willing to turn from my sin and commit my life to Jesus?*

- *Do I believe that Jesus died for my sins and was raised from the dead (Acts 1:22, 2:24)?*

IF YOU HAVE NOT YET COMMITTED YOUR LIFE TO JESUS, DON'T WAIT; DO IT NOW.

Have the intention to turn from your sin. Confess that you believe Jesus died for your sins and was raised from the dead. Tell Him you want Him to be your Lord and Savior.

4) Read Romans 10:10–13

a) Verse 10: What is the outcome of believing?

b) Verse 10: What is the outcome of confessing Jesus as Lord?

c) Verses 11 & 13: What are God's promises?

d) Verse 12: Who is this promise for?

Isn't God's Word very clear concerning the simplicity of the gospel? It has nothing to do with being Jewish or Gentile. It has nothing to do with what so-called Christian religion you may have been raised in. It has nothing to do with works! It is all about faith! We are told how man believes to righteousness but naturally confesses out loud to salvation. It is normal for one to believe and then confess what they believe, as only a liar would confess something they did not believe.

We are again told how faith, not works, results in receiving God's righteousness. This is how one is justified. We are also shown the importance of expressing (Proverbs 18:21; Matthew 10:32; Luke 12:8) and confessing Jesus as Lord (Acts 2:36; 1 Corinthians 8:6). Know that there is a responsibility to act on your belief. Paul tells how God's promise of salvation (justification) is simple, as anyone who calls and believes in the name of the Lord will be saved. This includes both Jew and Gentile (Acts 26:16–18) and is also available to those who are not spiritual Israel (Romans 9:6). It is imperative to know that God does not turn anyone away. Paul also puts to rest anyone still questioning whether salvation is by works or faith (Isaiah 28:16).

Notice how, in verse 13, Paul quotes Joel, who used *Yahweh* for the word *'Lord'* (Joel 2:32): Why is this important? Paul states that Jesus and Yahweh are One (Acts 2:21; Romans 9:5).

◆ ◆ ◆

Verses 14–17

The importance of giving the gospel.

5) Read Romans 10:14–17

a) Verse 14: What is the answer to Paul's three questions?

b) Verse 15: What are we told about those who preach the gospel?

c) Verse 16: What are we told about those who hear the gospel?

d) Verse 17: How does one receive faith?

There are three keys to an individual coming to saving faith in Jesus. One must first hear the gospel (Acts 8:31–39), then decide to put their faith in the gospel, and then confess Jesus as Lord. Hence, it is important for a believer to preach the gospel to a non-believer. Paul does not state that one gets saved by the example of a Christian. He does not state that one gets saved by befriending a non-believer with the hope that after a while, they will accept *your* Jesus. He states one gets saved by first hearing the gospel (Romans 1:15–16). The sovereign God not only calls those into the ministry (Ephesians 4:11), but also equips and sends His children to go into the world and preach the good news (Matthew 28:19; Mark 16:15).

What are Christians equipped with? The gospel (Acts 14:21). We are told how those who receive the gospel do so with joy! Since it is the gospel that does its work in believers (1 Thessalonians 2:13), the result is that all the glory goes to God, who alone causes the growth (1 Corinthians 3:6–7).

The prophets declared not only the importance of preaching the gospel (Isaiah 52:7; Nahum 1:15), but also that it is good news that brings joy to those who accept it. Know that only a gospel without works could do this (Ephesians 2:8–9). Most hear a different gospel, one which places burdens on people but does not promise salvation or result in joy. Remember that while not everyone is called to be an evangelist (Ephesians 4:11), all Christians are called to evangelize (Ephesians 6:15), that is, preach the good news to anyone who will listen (Psalm 19:4; Acts 26:16–18).

Notice how Paul states that not all heeded the good news. Isn't this crazy? Isn't the gospel simple? How does one reject what God makes so clear? The rejection by the Jews should not have come as a surprise, as it was prophesied over seven hundred years before the time of Christ (Isaiah 53:1). We have already been told how only spiritual Israel will respond to the gospel (John 8:37; Romans 9:6; 1 Corinthians 1:18).

Why is it so important to give the gospel? Because God's Word delivers faith. Let me repeat this. Only God's Word delivers faith, which is a gift (Ephesians 2:8–9). The result is every good thing we have is, in fact, a gift from God (James 1:17). The good news is Christians are simply called to deliver Scripture that contains the gospel (John 3:16). Let me point out how just as one goes to a doctor and receives medicine when sick, the world is sick with sin and the only cure is the gospel.

Know that salvation is a sovereign act of God accomplished by His Word. Jesus created us (Colossians 1:16), chose us (Titus 1:1), died for us, and gave us the faith necessary for salvation. It is Jesus alone who saves! The result is that Jesus gets all the glory as He is the Word (John 1:1) and the way (John 14:6). Paul understood this very well, stating that he endured all things knowing that the gospel is not imprisoned and it would bear fruit in those chosen (2 Timothy 2:10–11). Knowing this truth, it is easy to understand how the Lord states that all Christians have been entrusted with the gospel (1 Thessalonians 2:4).

Verses 18–21

The non-belief of Israel.

6) Read Romans 10:18–21

a) Verse 18: Have the Jews heard the gospel?

b) Verse 19: What did God promise for their rejection?

c) Verse 20: What did Isaiah state would happen?

d) Verse 21: What about Israel?

Paul now deals with the hypothetical question: Did the Jews even hear the good news? He stressed how they have heard the gospel (Psalm 19:4) and witnessed miracles performed by Jesus (John 12:37), including the raising of Lazarus (John 11:43-48), yet they still rejected Him. The Jews were also entrusted with the oracles of God (Romans 3:2). They had prophets who told of the coming Messiah. Despite this, many of them rejected the gospel (Acts 13:46, 18:6), even though it was first brought to them just as the prophet Isaiah had told them it would happen (Isaiah 53:1).

Paul now deals with a second hypothetical question: Did Israel understand what they were rejecting (Deuteronomy 32:21)? Did they know that God also intended the Gentiles for salvation? God foretold through many of the prophets that the Gentiles were included in His plan for salvation (Isaiah 11:10, 28:16, 49:6, 56:6-7, 63:16; Joel 2:32; Malachi 1:11; Hosea 1:10, 2:23).

The nation of Israel's rejection of Messiah was foretold (Isaiah 49:7, 53:3). They rejected the Messiah even though Daniel prophesied to the very day He would be revealed (Daniel 9:25), with the result of their rejection being the fall of Jerusalem (Zechariah 11:6; Luke 19:44). Jesus told how the kingdom would be taken away and given to another that produces fruit (Matthew 21:41–44). Paul cites both Moses (Deuteronomy 32:21) and Isaiah (Isaiah 65:1), pointing out how the Jews even missed the fact that the Lord promised He would make them jealous by calling the Gentiles. Notice how God balances that statement by telling how He has continually opened His hands to the nation of Israel (Isaiah 65:2). While Israel has rejected God, He continues to patiently await her.

Will Israel continue in non-belief? The next chapter gives us God's answer.

CHAPTER ELEVEN

God is not through with Israel.

Verses 1–10

Despite her rejection of Jesus, God is certainly not through with Israel.

1) Read Romans 11:1–6

    a) Verse 1: What question is asked?

    b) Verses 1 & 2: What is God's answer?

    c) Verse 1: What fact does Paul use to confirm this?

    d) Verses 2 & 3: What second example does he use to confirm this?

    e) Verse 4: How did God respond to Elijah?

    f) Verse 5: How did Paul apply God's words to Elijah in his own time?

    g) Verse 5: Who is responsible for this remnant?

    h) Verse 6: What is God's choice based on?

    i) Verse 6: What is salvation not based on?

j) Verse 6: Can grace be called grace if salvation is by works?

Contrary to what many teach, and despite the Jews' rejection of God, Paul tells how He has not discarded or wholly rejected the nation of Israel.

What evidence does Paul use to confirm this truth? First, the fact that he is a Christian Jew from the small insignificant tribe of Benjamin (Acts 9:1–22; Philippians 3:5). The second example Paul uses is Elijah, who was a prophet to the idolatrous nation of Israel (1 Kings 19).

What do we know about Elijah? During his ministry, the northern Kingdom of Israel was very idolatrous. Baal worship was prevalent throughout the entire kingdom under King Ahab and his wicked queen Jezebel. The Lord responded to the people's idolatry by raising the prophet Elijah, whose mission would be to reveal the identity of the one true God and begin the extermination of Baalism in Israel. When Elijah killed the prophets of Baal (1 Kings 18:40), he mistakenly thought that he had put an end to this pagan worship. He became so discouraged by Jezebel's response to these events that he abandoned his duty and asked the Lord to let him die, concluding that he had failed and was left alone as a follower of the God of Israel.

This fear caused him to flee to the southernmost part of Judah, where he was first fed by an angel and then spent forty days at Horeb without food. The gentle God of the Bible responded by instructing him to go north to Damascus, calmly telling him to anoint Elisha as his successor (1 Kings 19:15–16). Elisha would then anoint Hazael, the future king of Aram, and Jehu, the future king of Israel. It was at this time that the Lord informed Elijah that He still had seven thousand men preserved for Himself in Israel (1 Kings 19:18).

Paul used this example to show how the Lord will preserve a remnant of Israel with the key being all according to His choice (Romans 11:5). This was exemplified in the early church by numerous Jews becoming saved (Acts 2:4, 4:4), even including priests (Acts 6:7). Keep in mind that Paul earlier stated that not all Israel is spiritual Israel (Romans 9:6–7). That being said, remember God clearly tells of the future restoration and salvation of Israel (Zechariah 12:10–11; Jeremiah 33:19–22).

Paul had just stated how Israel did not attain the needed righteousness because they pursued it by works and not by faith (Romans 9:30–33). The result is seeking to establish your own righteousness, refusing Christ's righteousness (Romans 10:3). God tells how the present remnant is according to His choice, stating that being one of the chosen is a gift not attained by works. Realize that God's Word clearly defines grace, saying that if salvation were by works, then grace would not be a gift but rather a wage (Romans 4:4). The result is that those chosen cannot boast of having anything to do with their salvation (2 Thessalonians 2:13; Ephesians 2:8–9; 1 Corinthians 4:7). The truth of God's grace leaves mankind with a decision to make.

Is salvation by grace, or is it by works? The good news is that God's Word gives us the answer!

2) Read Romans 11:7–10

a) Verse 7: Which Jews have salvation?

b) Verse 7: What about the rest of Israel?

c) Verse 8: How was this foretold by Moses?

d) Verses 9 & 10: How did David confirm this?

The natural question is, what about the rest of the Jews? Paul summarizes his argument by saying that those who were not chosen were judicially hardened. The result reveals the identity of spiritual Israel. Paul tells how the fact that God has hardened some should not come as a surprise, as the Lord had previously hardened the Jews for their disbelief. Know that all who refuse or resist Jesus potentially face the same fate (Hebrews 4:7). Just like Pharaoh was hardened by his sin (Exodus 8:15, 9:34), those who reject Jesus are hardening their hearts.

Paul first quotes Moses telling how the Jews had failed to respond to the Lord (Deuteronomy 29:4). This is even though they witnessed the Exodus, had been sustained with the manna from Heaven, were given water from a rock, and had the Shekinah glory of God to lead them. Paul combines this Scripture with Isaiah (Isaiah 29:10), foretelling how the Lord would respond to those He described as those who only honored Him with their lips while their heart was far from Him. By doing so, Paul states that these events should not come as a surprise since they were foretold in the Old Testament. Isaiah told how the people's reverence for Him was tradition and was learned by rote, that is, external and legislated (Isaiah 29:10–14).

To further make his point, Paul quotes David's Messianic prophecy (Psalm 69:22–26). The context of this psalm is David praying that his enemies would stumble over their blessings. Paul uses these Scriptures to explain that the Jews thought themselves chosen, so they stumbled over their spiritual blessings (the Law and the prophets, which pointed to Christ), ultimately rejecting the Messiah whom they persecuted. The result was God bringing upon the Jews exactly what David had prayed would happen to those who persecuted him. The Jews were trusting in their external religious rituals, which led them to judgment, not realizing that the Law was only to be their tutor until the arrival of the Messiah (Galatians 3:24).

Isn't this what religion does? It substitutes rituals for the substance (Colossians 2:17), which is a personal relationship with God through Jesus Christ (John 17:3; 1 John 5:20; 2 Thessalonians 1:8).

Isn't this exactly what the Roman Catholic Church teaches? I was trained to recite prayers over and over. I was taught I had to go to mass, which was a time of repeating prayers accompanied by times of sitting, standing, and kneeling. I was also taught God was impersonal and incapable of having a personal relationship with someone like me.

How can I say this? I was taught that I could not even confess my sins to Jesus directly because anyone desiring reconciliation with God needed to confess their sins to a priest (Catechism 1493) who himself forgives sin as a judge (Catechism 1442, 1461). I was also taught the ridiculous heresy that even if a priest was deprived of his faculties of hearing, he could still absolve every sin (Catechism 1463).

❖ ❖ ❖

Verses 11–24

The Jews' rejection of Jesus is only temporary.

3) Read Romans 11:11–15

a) Verse 11: What does Paul say about the Jews stumbling?

b) Verse 11: What has happened as a result of the Jews rejecting Messiah?

c) Verse 11: Why?

d) Verse 12: What is the result?

e) Verse 13: Whom is Paul talking to?

f) Verse 13: How does Paul describe himself?

g) Verse 14: What was Paul's goal?

h) Verse 15: What is the fruit of Israel's rejection of Jesus?

i) Verse 15: How is Israel's future acceptance of Jesus described?

Notice how Paul states that the Jews have stumbled but not fallen. The fact that there were Jewish believers at this time proves his point (Romans 11:1). We are told how God allowed Israel to stumble in order for salvation to come to the Gentiles. The rejection of the Messiah is what caused Paul to turn from the Jews to the Gentiles (Acts 13:46, 18:6). Again, this should have come as no surprise, as the Old Testament foretold how the Gentiles would be saved (Genesis 12:3; Isaiah 49:6).

Paul tells the Gentiles of a future time when the Jews will return. Make no mistake about this: God's Word foretells how the Jews will return to their Lord (Jeremiah 31:35–37; Zechariah 12:10, 13:1; Revelation 7:4). Even though Paul knew that his primary mission was to be the apostle to the Gentiles (Acts 9:15, 21:19, 22:21; Galatians 2:8), his goal was to make the non-believing Jews jealous and turn their hearts toward the Lord. It is so sad that present-day Christians fail to have the same attitude toward non-believing Jewish people. Know that whenever anyone turns to the Messiah, they pass from death to life (John 5:24; Colossians 2:13). Ezekiel describes the day when the Lord will make the Jews alive when they will turn to the Messiah (Ezekiel 37:1–14).

4) Read Romans 11:16–18

a) Verse 16: What are we told about the first fruit and root being holy?

b) Verse 17: What are we told about some of the branches?

c) Verse 17: How are Gentiles described?

d) Verse 17: What happened to the Gentiles?

e) Verse 18: What is our attitude toward the Jews to be?

f) Verse 18: Why?

When Paul refers to the first part of the dough as being holy, he is probably referring to the Feast of First Fruits. This was a time when Jews were required to offer their first fruits of the earth—grain (Leviticus 23:9–14) and cakes made from them (Numbers 15:17–21). These were offered to the Lord, with the result being a blessing on the rest of their house. If the first part of the dough was holy, the rest would also be holy.

The Feast of First Fruits was a feast that occurred the day after the Sabbath that followed Passover. It was a time when the Jews would take a sheaf of the first part of the barley harvest and offer it to the Lord. Acceptance by the Lord was viewed as Him sanctifying their entire harvest. It is interesting to note that Jesus rose from the dead on the same day the first fruits were offered. This was not a coincidence! Paul confronted heretics who stated there was no resurrection (1 Corinthians 15:12–14) by telling how Christ is the first fruit of those who are asleep (1 Corinthians 15:20–23), using this metaphor to assure Christians of their future resurrection.

Exactly who is the first piece? The believing Jews, from Abraham, Isaac, and Jacob, are also described as a cultivated olive tree (Jeremiah 11:16). Paul states that the Lord's acceptance of Abraham ensures acceptance of his seed. Remember, the apostles were Jews, and the first Christians were Jews (Acts 2:5, 41).

Who is the root? While some believe that the patriarchs are the root, I believe that Jesus is the root (Revelation 5:5, 22:16).

Paul tells how some of the branches were broken off, and wild olives (the Gentiles) were grafted in. The fact that not all of the branches were broken off for their non-belief confirms the earlier statement that God has not rejected Israel and still has a remnant of Jews (Romans 11:2–5). While the olive tree is spiritual Israel (Romans 9:6), God does not differentiate between Jews and Gentiles in the body of Christ (Galatians 3:28). Know that God has not replaced Israel with Gentiles.

Let me repeat: God has not cut down the old tree and replaced it with a new one. Salvation is of the Jews through the Messiah (John 4:22). This is why Paul tells us that we are not to be arrogant toward non-believing Jews. Christians should not be arrogant toward any non-believer because the only reason we are saved is by God's grace. Jesus is the root who gives life and sustains all believers. He is the vine, and we are the branches (John 15:5).

5) Read Romans 11:19–20

a) Verse 19: What truth is repeated?

b) Verse 20: Why were branches broken off?

c) Verse 20: What enables Gentiles to stand?

d) Verse 20: What should the result be?

Paul reiterates the fact that salvation is not by works but rather faith (Habakkuk 2:4). While it is true that branches (Jews) were broken off for their disbelief, Gentiles need to realize that the only reason they have been grafted in is due to God's mercy and choice (Romans 11:6). We have done nothing that warranted our salvation.

How were we grafted in? By our faith, which is a gift of God (Ephesians 2:8), we are delivered by hearing His Word (Romans 10:17). This truth should cause great humility in any believer. That being said, do not confuse boasting with faith, which is simply trusting in the promises of God.

6) Read Romans 11:21–24

a) Verse 21: What will happen to those who boast and lack faith?

b) Verse 22: What two things are we told about our just God?

c) Verse 22: What qualification is given?

d) Verse 23: Who does the grafting into the olive tree?

e) Verse 24: What olive trees were the unbelieving Jews and Gentiles cut off from?

f) Verse 24: What are we told about this process?

g) Verse 24: Is it difficult for God to graft in the Jews?

Paul warns the Gentiles (not individually) that just as easily as God cut off the Jews, He could also do the same with them. Boasting is rooted in pride, which is often combined with a lack of faith in the one true God.

Who was not spared? The non-believing Jews.

Who was shown kindness? The Gentiles.

How? Their faith in Jesus.

This kindness was not a reaction to the unbelief of the Jews, as it was always part of God's plan (Genesis 12:1–3). Paul again emphasizes the importance of faith, not works. Faith is what saves one from the severity of God (Proverbs 28:14). And notice how Paul again underscores the importance of perseverance (Romans 2:7; 1 Timothy 4:16), which can only be accomplished by abiding in Jesus (John 15:1–8). Only those who continue in the faith until the end of their life are genuine believers (Hebrews 3:6, 14), and abiding faith is proof of one's salvation. The grafting God has done, which is contrary to nature, illustrates how He brings people into His family through faith.

What do we know about a wild, uncultivated olive tree? Even if it does produce fruit, it will be small and worthless.

What do we know about a cultivated olive tree? It has a sturdy and extensive root system that supports the entire tree. It also bears good fruit.

What makes this unique is God telling how He has grafted a wild olive branch into a good olive tree. This is the opposite of normally taking a good branch and grafting it into a wild tree. God did not create a new tree. He did not desert the old tree by taking a branch from the good tree and grafting it into a wild tree. He simply (and supernaturally) grafted Gentiles (Ephesians 2:12–16) into the good tree (spiritual Israel) that He created.

By being grafted in, Gentiles now receive the blessings promised to Abraham, Isaac, and Jacob, all of which come through the Messiah. Paul deals with any doctrine teaching that God is through with Israel by telling how easily the Lord can and will graft the (natural olive branch) Jews back into the olive tree. Notice how this will not require breaking off Gentile branches. There is plenty of room on the good olive tree to accommodate all who trust in Christ, both Jews and Gentiles.

❖ ❖ ❖

Verses 25–32

Israel will be restored.

7) Read Romans 11:25–27

a) Verse 25: What has happened to Israel?

b) Verse 25: When will this cease?

c) Verses 26 & 27: What will happen?

While Paul confirms that Israel has been hardened (Romans 11:7–8), he clarifies this by saying that it is only a partial hardening that does not include all Jews. We have also been told that this hardening is temporary.

Exactly when will the hardening of the Jews be removed? While God does not give us the answer, He does state it will not be until the fullness of the Gentiles is fulfilled. That is, there is a specific number of Gentiles (elect) who will be saved during a time frame that only God knows. When that number and time are complete, the fullness of the Gentiles will be complete.

One of the curses for disobedience to the Law was Israel (described as the tail) being led by an alien (described as a head) (Deuteronomy 28:43–44). This has been fulfilled since the Babylonian invasion of Judah (586 BC), which was followed by domination by the Medo-Persian, Greek, and Roman Empires. After the fall of Jerusalem (70 AD), the Jews were scattered until May 14th of 1948, when the nation of Israel was re-established (Isaiah 66:18), and they did not control Jerusalem until 1967. These events show how the amazing process of restoration has begun.

The fact that Jesus mentioned the times of the Gentiles being fulfilled (Luke 21:23–24) tells us that there is a time appointed when this will happen. This time will likely end when the last kingdom described by the prophet Daniel (Daniel 2:40), and more specifically, when the little horn who arises from the beast (Daniel 7:8) comes against Israel in the tribulation period. While one might argue that this time passed with the Jews capturing Jerusalem, the presence of the Dome of the Rock and the fact that the city will be trodden down with Gentiles during the tribulation period tell how fulfillment remains in the future (Revelation 11:2).

While there is presently a remnant of believing Jews, God tells of a future time when all of Israel (those predestined) will be saved by the Deliverer who will come to Zion and remove all ungodliness (Isaiah 59:20–21; 2 Samuel 5:7). Know that Paul is not referring to all Jews from all time but rather to those alive from the nation that will see Him and believe. This time will fulfill Jeremiah's prophecy concerning the New Covenant God has with His people (Jeremiah 31:33–34).

Paul tells how the fullness of Gentiles might end with Jesus being revealed (Isaiah 59:20). While some believe the timing of this is at the end of the tribulation period (which is 3 1/2 years), I believe it could be right before the great tribulation begins as foretold by the prophet Zechariah (Zechariah 12:10–11), described as a time when the Jews will look on Him whom they have pierced. It very well might also coincide with the Lord rescuing Israel from a coming invasion (Ezekiel 38), resulting in the nation recognizing Jesus as their Messiah and Lord (Ezekiel 39:22). We do know that He will come out of heavenly Jerusalem and remove their sins (Isaiah 27:9; Hebrews 8:12). We don't have to know the exact timing to believe that the God who has made these promises will act in His time.

8) Read Romans 11:28–31

a) Verse 28: Who are described as enemies of the gospel?

b) Verse 28: Why are they still beloved?

c) Verse 29: What about the sovereignty of God?

d) Verse 30: How are we described before we became Christians?

e) Verse 30: What have we been shown and why?

f) Verse 31: To whom will God ultimately show mercy?

While Paul describes the non-believing Jews as enemies of the gospel, this title belongs to all non-believers who are also described as enemies of God (Romans 5:10). Despite this, they are still beloved for the sake of their forefathers. God is and will continue to be faithful to the promises He made to the patriarchs.

There are many examples of the faithfulness of God for the sake of His promises. For instance, the Lord told Isaac He would bless him for the sake of Abraham (Genesis 26:24). He told Solomon He would not tear the kingdom in his days for the sake of David (1 Kings 11:12–13), the Lord endured Rehoboam's wicked son Abijam for three years for the sake of David (1 Kings 15:1–5), and through Isaiah, the Lord told Hezekiah that He would defend Jerusalem for the sake of David (2 Kings 19:34).

This is also exemplified by Moses telling how the Lord did not choose the Jews because they were special (Deuteronomy 7:7–9, 10:15), but rather because of the oath He made to their fathers long before they could be called a nation. This reveals God's faithfulness and confirms that the gifts and calling of God are irrevocable. God is faithful to His promises concerning Israel, and this despite their unfaithfulness.

Why does God keep the promises that He has made? Because He never changes (Malachi 3:6). This is why He did not destroy the Jews when they turned from Him to idols. Remember that this character trait allows us to trust in Him as it is impossible for Him to lie (Hebrews 6:18). Know that God has shown and will continue to show mercy toward the nation of Israel. He is not finished with the Jews!

Paul reminds us how we Gentiles have a responsibility to the unsaved Jews (Romans 11:11–14). Just as the disobedient Gentiles were shown mercy because of the Jews' rejection of the Messiah, the mercy shown to the Gentiles should be used to bring the Jews to Christ.

Verses 32–36

What, how, and why God has done what He has done.

9) Read Romans 11:32–36

a) Verse 32: What has God done?

b) Verse 32: Why?

c) Verses 33-35: How does Paul react to this truth?

d) Verse 36: What is the result?

While everyone (Jew and Gentile) has been disobedient to God, He planned to stress this fact with the result of shutting every mouth. While this seems harsh, it shows His great mercy.

How did God shut every mouth? The Mosaic Law, as the result of being under it, confirms our being a slave to sin (Romans 6:14). We know that everyone is born into this world under the Law.

What is the result? God has shut up everyone in disobedience so He could show mercy to all (Galatians 3:22).

Through the Law, God has ensured that everyone knows they are sinners in need of a Savior. The result should be a greater desire to have a Savior. Realizing this truth about the Law, Paul marvels at the wisdom and mercy of God. He needs no one to advise or counsel Him (Isaiah 40:13–14). In fact, He needs nothing from His creation, who has been given everything (Job 35:7, 41:11). The result is He owes no one anything as all have sinned and fall short of His glory (Romans 3:23). In fact, all of Creation owes its very existence to Jesus Christ (Colossians 1:16). From the beginning of time, God has had a plan, with the result being a redeemed and godly chosen people (Ephesians 2:7) who will praise Him forever (Ephesians 1:6).

CHAPTER TWELVE

How to apply God's mercies to our lives.

Verses 1–2

How to apply the mercies of God to the way we live.

1) Read Romans 12:1–2

    a) Verse 1: What are Christians instructed to do?

    b) Verse 1: What allows us to do so?

    c) Verse 2: What are we told not to do?

    d) Verse 2: How do we avoid the mistake?

    e) Verse 2: What will this reveal?

    Reflecting on God's mercies that were described in the previous chapter, Paul uses the word, "therefore," to urge Christians to respond by completely presenting themselves to God (Romans 6:13, 19), reminding us it is only rational or reasonable to do so (1 Corinthians 6:20). Realize this bodily presentation is something the worship of a Christian should always include.

    Paul had earlier described our unrighteousness (Romans 3:23), that we deserved death for our sin (Romans 6:23), that God had shut us up in disobedience to show us mercy (Romans 11:32), that our justification was a gift (Romans 5:1), that we have been set free from sin's power (Romans 6:14), that we are not condemned for our sins (Romans 8:1), that we were chosen before the beginning of time (Romans 8:29–30), and that nothing can separate us from the love of God (Romans 8:38-39). In addition, all Christians have been purchased by God (Acts 20:28; Revelation 5:9).

Knowing these truths, we should understand Paul is making perfect sense in imploring us to present ourselves as a living sacrifice to God. Keep in mind that there are only two sacrifices mentioned in the entire New Testament that are expected of us! These are the sacrifice of presenting ourselves to our Lord and the sacrifice of praise (Hebrews 13:15).

This is opposite to what the present-day Catholic Church teaches, stating that the mass is an ongoing bloodless sacrifice (Catechism 1367, 1382) offered for the living and the dead in order to obtain spiritual benefits from God (Catechism 1414). The heresy being taught is that one must do something in order to receive the mercies of God (Titus 3:5). This is so wrong because God's mercies are free and new every day (Lamentations 3:22–23), obtained by the one sacrifice of Jesus on the cross of Calvary. Paul had earlier told us to present ourselves to God as one alive from the dead (Romans 6:13). We are now beseeched to give ourselves completely to Jesus to be used as His instrument on this earth.

How do we give ourselves completely to Jesus? By not conforming to the world (1 Peter 1:14; 1 John 2:15) and by renewing our mind (2 Corinthians 3:18). This is how we keep our commitment. The key to a renewed mind is focusing on God's Word, which instructs us about how the inner man is being renewed through the process of sanctification (2 Corinthians 4:16).

How is our mind renewed? By cleansing the individual who reads God's Word and puts it into practice (Ephesians 5:26; James 1:22–25). Thus, Christians are being renewed to the true knowledge according to the image of God (Colossians 3:10).

Many Christians are so involved in their ministry or service that they fail to take the time to be transformed. We are to renew our mind, which is accomplished by laying aside our old self (1 John 2:15; Ephesians 4:23). Christians have a responsibility to take an active part in their sanctification. How much and how fast you change to be more like Christ is directly related to the amount of time you spend in God's Word and prayer (2 Corinthians 3:18). Just as we should reckon ourselves as dead to sin (Romans 6:11), those desiring change should daily offer themselves to God. This includes praying for His will in our lives (Matthew 6:10). The transformation that follows will prove God's will in our lives.

What is God's will? Our sanctification (1 Thessalonians 4:3) and giving thanks for what we have been given (1 Thessalonians 5:18).

◆ ◆ ◆

Verses 3–8

The different gifts in the Church.

2) Read Romans 12:3–8

a) Verse 3: How are Christians to act?

b) Verse 3: What has God given to each Christian?

c) Verse 4: What are we told about our natural body?

d) Verse 5: What are we told about the body of Christ?

e) Verse 6: What are we told about the gifts we have been given?

f) Verses 6-8: List the 7 different gifts that are mentioned and how they are to be used.

Paul invokes his authority, saying that in light of the mercies of God, we are to remain humble. Even today, many Christians think more highly of themselves than they should.

Why should we not boast? Because God has determined where we have been placed in the Body of Christ (1 Corinthians 12:11; James 2:5). Just as all members of our earthly body serve a function, God has placed Christians in different places with the specific purpose of glorifying Jesus Christ (1 Peter 4:10–11).

Notice that all Christians have been given a different proportion of faith (2 Thessalonians 3:2; 2 Peter 1:1); thus, we are not to pass judgment on those with less faith (Romans 14:1–2). Let me repeat this: We are not to pass judgment on those who have received less faith than our own (Ephesians 2:8-9; 1 Corinthians 12:9). We are to use our spiritual gifts to exhort and encourage those less mature in the faith. Remember that all Christians are instructed to pursue faith (1 Timothy 6:11; 2 Timothy 2:22), which increases in the knowledge of God and of Jesus Christ (2 Peter 1:2).

How does one increase their faith? Through God's Word and personal experiences of God's faithfulness (2 Corinthians 10:15).

Since God has determined those who are the most visible in the body of Christ (Ephesians 4:11), they should take heed, as they had nothing to do with this choice. This is why Paul tells us to exercise our gifts with a spirit of humility. Notice how the gifts that Paul mentions are all used for the benefit of building the Body of Christ (Ephesians 4:12). Realize that there can be a difference between the gifts an individual has been given and their current level of spiritual maturity. This is why it is so important not to look at man but rather at God! Know that spiritual maturity is directly related to the amount of time one spends in prayer and studying God's Word.

Imagine a very large lifeboat filled with all Christians from all time. This is a good analogy for who we are. Know that there is no spiritual hierarchy in this lifeboat because we are all sinners saved by grace. Paul knew very well that God is no respecter of persons (Galatians 2:6; Romans 2:11). Just as the world idolizes certain athletes who were simply born with their athleticism, Christians make the mistake of esteeming certain leaders who have been placed in prominent positions. Remember that it is only praise from God that matters, as He both knows (1 Corinthians 4:5; 2 Corinthians 5:10) and will judge the motives and secrets of the heart (Romans 2:16).

❖ ❖ ❖

Verses 9–21

The importance of love in Christian service.

3) Read Romans 12:9–11

a) Verse 9: What are we told to do?

b) Verse 9: What two attitudes will help us accomplish this goal?

c) Verse 10: What two actions reveal love without hypocrisy?

d) Verse 11: What are Christians exhorted to be?

e) Verse 11: What two choices will help prevent us from lagging behind?

We are exhorted to be sincere and not hypocritical in our actions toward other Christians, which can be exhibited when our deeds do not match our words (1 John 3:18). For example, James warned how some will dishonor the poor and show favoritism to the affluent Christians (James 2:1–3), not remembering we are all sinners saved by grace, and all Christians are brothers and sisters in the Lord (1 Timothy 5:1–2).

Instead of being hypocrites, we are told to abhor anything evil and cling to what is good (Psalm 97:10; Amos 5:15). Think about how one would hate something. They would avoid it, be revolted and disgusted by it, and try not to even think about it. This is how we should feel toward sin and evil. Many Christians hate how sin impacts them, but fail to hate sin itself. Just as the evil hate the light and do their best to avoid it (John 3:20), Christians should hate evil and do their best to avoid it.

How can we cling to what is good? By first having God's perspective about what is good (Titus 2:11–12). This is accomplished by examining everything carefully and abstaining from evil (1 Thessalonians 5:21–22). The result is devotion to others in brotherly love and regarding others as more important than ourselves (Philippians 2:1–4). Remember, the Body of Christ is made up of all believers.

Love should be the motivation for our lives. This means not only love toward Jesus and our brothers and sisters in the Lord (Mark 12:30–31) but also love for those who hate us (Luke 6:27-28, 23:34). Paul tells how brotherly devotion is exhibited by giving preference to one another in honor. These actions reveal the genuineness of our faith and fulfill part of the royal law (Matthew 22:36–39; James 2:8). Remember that all followers of Jesus should be distinguished by their love (John 13:35; 1 John 3:14). Love is one of the fruits of the Spirit and is exhibited by things like patience (Galatians 5:22–23), kindness, gentleness, and self-control.

Why is love, in fact, greater than any other spiritual gift? Because one can practice love using whatever gift one possesses. Paul told the Corinthians of the importance of love (1 Corinthians 13:4–7), making the point that works done without love profit nothing (1 Corinthians 13:2–3). Jesus told us how the spiritual service we do for others will be counted as being done to Him (Matthew 25:35–40).

Notice how Paul exhorts us to be diligent and fervent in our service to the Lord. Many times, Christians can become complacent, forgetting how it is only due to the grace of God that we are saved (Ephesians 2:8–9). The knowledge of God's grace should encourage us to want to glorify and serve our Savior, remembering that our time on this earth is short (Psalm 90:12).

4) Read Romans 12:12

a) What are we to rejoice in?

b) What will this help us do?

c) What else is the key to persevering?

No matter what happens, Christians should always have an eternal perspective. Doing so will help encourage perseverance. We are told to rejoice in the sure hope we have (Philippians 4:4; 1 Thessalonians 5:16; Hebrews 6:19), which is akin to putting on the helmet of salvation (1 Thessalonians 5:8). This must also include times of trials (James 1:1–3).

How do we rejoice in hope? In prayer, we exult in the promises of God (2 Corinthians 1:20; 2 Peter 1:4) and the fact that we were chosen by Him (Romans 8:29; Ephesians 1:5).

All Christians should fix their hope on our Savior Jesus Christ (1 Timothy 1:1, 4:10), who has promised us eternal life (Titus 1:2). This rejoicing is a sure sign of our salvation (Psalm 116:12–13). Know that even reading God's Word alone should cause joy (Psalm 119:11; Jeremiah 15:16). The Bible gives the same command concerning rejoicing in dozens of places (Psalm 31:7; 2 Corinthians 13:11). Realize that our rejoicing in the Lord pleases Him and doing so brings Him great glory (Psalm 147:11).

Why is rejoicing in the Lord so important? Because God's Word tells us how doing so will remove our anxiety, give us peace, and guard our hearts (Philippians 4:4–7).

While we were without hope before we came to know the Lord (Ephesians 2:12; 1 Thessalonians 4:13), all Christians now have eternal life (1 John 2:25) promised by our God who cannot lie (Hebrews 6:18). This realization should cause us to rejoice even more, helping us persevere in our trials and tribulations (Philippians 3:1; Romans 5:3–4). Most Christians don't fully understand the prize awaiting those who place their faith in Jesus (1 Corinthians 2:9; Philippians 3:14).

The hope we have in Jesus is what encourages us to pray, with the result being our peace and increased understanding. Notice how Christians are instructed not only to pray but also to be devoted to prayer. God's will is for us to pray without ceasing (1 Thessalonians 5:17–18), giving thanks for the blessings we have received. We should continually support each other through our prayers (Colossians 1:9; Ephesians 6:18), knowing that such prayers are always answered (Mark 11:24).

5) Read Romans 12:13–16

a) Verses 13, 15. & 16: How are we to treat the saints?

b) Verse 14: How are we to act toward non-believers?

c) Verse 16: What are we warned not to do?

We are implored to practice hospitality, which includes not only emotional support of but also contributing to the needs of the saints (1 Corinthians 16:15). Realize that our Lord will remember these deeds even if no one else notices (Hebrews 6:10; Proverbs 3:3–4). When even one member suffers, the entire Body of Christ suffers with it (1 Corinthians 12:26). That is why supporting and exhorting each other in good times and also times of trials is not only necessary (Colossians 3:12–13; 1 Thessalonians 2:11) but also reveals the love we have for each other.

Christians should also pray for their enemies (Matthew 5:44; Luke 6:28), knowing that this will also help us endure during our times of trials (1 Corinthians 4:12). Notice how we are told not to be impartial toward other believers (Acts 10:34). This includes those who are considered lowly by the world. This should mean intentional times of rejoicing and weeping with other believers. Because all Christians are saved by grace and not by works (Ephesians 2:8–9), there is no reason to boast.

I previously brought up the illustration of a very large lifeboat in the middle of the ocean. Know that in that lifeboat, there are no titles except "sinner saved by grace." There are no individuals elevated over others. This is why we are also told not to be conceited or even consider ourselves wise (Proverbs 3:7). Every good thing we have has been given to us by God (James 1:17; Ephesians 1:3). This not only includes the faith we have (Romans 12:3) but even the works we do on this earth (Ephesians 2:10). Remember that no one can boast in their knowledge of the Lord because one only knows what God has chosen to reveal to us (Matthew 16:17; Luke 24:45; 1 John 5:20).

6) Read Romans 12:17–18

a) Verse 17: How are we to respond to evil?

b) Verse 17: Why is this important?

c) Verse 18: What are we encouraged to do?

Paul now discusses the relationship that Christians should have with their enemies. Know that the context of this is in Christian service. Unlike what the world believes and expects, Christians are to respond in love to evil by turning the other cheek (Matthew 5:38–45). These actions were first modeled by Jesus, who did not retaliate (Matthew 26:67–68) but allowed Himself to be beaten, spit upon, and mocked (Isaiah 53:7).

Just as Jesus was closely watched (Mark 3:2; Luke 14:1, 20:20), the actions of Christians are also noticed by all men (2 Corinthians 3:2; 1 Peter 2:12). This is why we are to be on our best behavior at all times. Remember, we are ambassadors for Christ as we represent Him on this earth (2 Corinthians 5:20). By responding to evil in a godly manner, we don't harm our ability to give the gospel to others. No matter what the circumstances, Christians are implored to live their life doing the right thing (Proverbs 3:1–4).

While Christians are encouraged to be at peace with all men, this will naturally depend on whether the other parties' attitudes are the same. While believers are always encouraged to work out their differences (1 Corinthians 6:5), there will be times when the gospel itself will even separate families (Matthew 10:35). That being said, giving the gospel should always be done in love (Ephesians 4:15), knowing that many will still refuse the grace of God (2 Thessalonians 2:10).

7) Read Romans 12:19–21

a) Verse 19: What are we encouraged not to do?

b) Verse 19: What truth can we rest in?

c) Verse 20: How are we to treat our enemies?

d) Verse 20: What is the result?

e) Verse 21: What are we exhorted to do?

f) Verse 21: How do we accomplish this?

Christians should never take revenge because it is Jesus alone who will impartially judge (Deuteronomy 32:35; Matthew 16:27; 1 Peter 1:17). We don't know if the revelation of our love will affect a non-believer (2 Kings 6:22). Even if it doesn't (Proverbs 20:22, 25:21–22), we can take solace in the fact that God's wrath will punish the guilty. Thus, the individual who fails to respond to the kindness shown them will result in God's judgment, described as burning coals (2 Samuel 22:9; Psalm 140:9–10).

Paul finishes the chapter by imploring us not to be overcome by evil but rather to use the good he has discussed to overcome evil. Allowing ourselves to take revenge would be one way we could be overcome by evil. Living our lives with love toward not only believers (1 Corinthians 16:14), but also our enemies (Luke 6:27–32) will fulfill the royal law (Leviticus 19:18; Galatians 5:14; James 2:8).

CHAPTER THIRTEEN

The way that Christians should conduct themselves.

Verses 1–7

The responsibility of a Christian is to obey the civil authorities.

1) Read Romans 13:1–3

a) Verse 1: To whom are Christians to be subject?

b) Who established the authority in our lives?

c) Verse 2: What are we told about those who disobey?

d) Verse 3: What are we told about the authorities in our lives?

e) Verse 3: What is the result of obedience?

In the previous chapter, Paul discussed the relationship Christians have with God, other Christians, and their enemies. He now discusses the relationship Christians are to have with their government, which also includes paying taxes (Matthew 22:21). Keep in mind Paul was writing to those in Rome at a time when the government was persecuting Christians.

While all Christians are to be in subjection to the government (Titus 3:1; 1 Peter 2:13–14), know this does not include times when the laws are clearly in conflict with the Laws of God (Daniel 3:4–6; Acts 5:28–29; Revelation 14:11). One reason Christians don't have to repay evil for evil is the fact that God uses the authority He has established to bring wrath on those who disobey (Romans 12:19). Paul tells how in a normal government, Christians have nothing to fear and will be praised for their obedience (1 Peter 2:14).

What about Christians who decide to obey God and disobey an evil government (Acts 4:19–20)? God will, at some point, be praised for their obedience (1 Peter 1:7, 2:12).

Why is disobeying the authorities rightfully placed in our lives equivalent to disobeying God Himself? Because God is a sovereign God of order (Daniel 4:17; John 19:11; 1 Corinthians 14:33). This truth is revealed by all of creation (Job 38, 39; Psalm 19:1; Nehemiah 9:6). Jesus determines which nations will be great (Job 12:23), their boundaries (Deuteronomy 32:8; Acts 17:26), and even the appointed times of man (Job 14:1–5). Jesus even determines who the leaders will be (Daniel 2:21).

We are often told that the God of the Bible demands His glory (Isaiah 42:8, 48:11). For instance, the Babylonian King Nebuchadnezzar was judged by God for three and a half years until he recognized that the Lord of the Bible is sovereign (Daniel 4:31–35). The Assyrian King Sennacherib proudly mocked the God of Israel, who then responded by telling him that he would be judged for his arrogance (2 Kings 19:10; Isaiah 37:23–25) because he was boastfully taking credit for what God had predetermined (Isaiah 37:26–29; Deuteronomy 32:39).

There are many examples of God's sovereignty. For example, God told how He raised the Babylonians to defeat the Assyrians and bring judgment on Judah (Habakkuk 1:5–6, 12; Nahum 2:6–10, 3:7; Isaiah 10:12). He also told how He would raise up the Medes to bring judgment on the Babylonians (Isaiah 13:17–19; Jeremiah 51:28–29).

In almost every civilization, people are not bothered if they obey. We are told how those who do not obey bring judgment on themselves. In some cases, that might even be capital punishment, which was first ordained by God (Genesis 9:5-6). The Greek word for *'condemnation'* used here is *krima* or *'judgment,'* not the Greek word *katakrima* or *'penalty'* previously used in this letter (Romans 8:1). Know it is for the Lord's sake that we submit to our leaders (1 Peter 2:13–15).

Knowing of God's authority structure, Paul appealed to the Roman government, using his Roman citizenship to obtain justice (Acts 16:37, 22:25). He also appealed to Festus, which prevented him from being turned over to the Sanhedrin (Acts 25:10–12), and enabled him to go to Rome where he would bear witness for Christ.

2) Read Romans 13:4–7

a) Verse 4: What are Christians warned about concerning disobedience?

b) Verse 5: Why is it necessary to be in subjection to the government?

c) Verse 6: What reason is given for the justification of paying taxes?

d) Verse 7: What are we exhorted to do?

Notice how these government officials are called "ministers" and equipped with the power to inflict punishment on those who disobey. By referring to the sword, Paul is discussing capital punishment (Genesis 9:6). Paul warns Christians how God has ordained and uses the government to punish those who disobey (1 Thessalonians 4:6). The result for Christians should not only be obedience but also not taking the law into their own hands, even if they feel justified in doing so. Murdering a doctor who performs abortions is a perfect example of what not to do, as vengeance belongs to the Lord alone (Romans 12:19).

The natural question might be, what about dishonest rulers who exceed God's will? While this frequently happens, know that they, too, will have to account to God. The prophet Zechariah told how the Lord was angry at the nations He raised to bring judgment to Judah (Zechariah 1:15). Why? Because they exceeded His will, ultimately bringing judgment upon themselves. The prophet Hosea told how Jehu's dynasty would not last (Hosea 1:4) because he exceeded God's will by killing Judah's King Ahaziah when God was judging Israel (2 Kings 9:16–28).

Christians are to be subjected to the authorities not only to avoid the wrath brought on by disobedience but also to have a clear conscience that is necessary if one is to be effective for the Lord (2 Timothy 1:3; Hebrews 9:14). Know that this subjection also includes paying taxes. Jesus modeled this by paying the two-drachma tax even though He would be exempt due to the fact that He was God's Son (Matthew 17:24–27). Jesus also told the disciples of the Pharisees to render to Caesar what belongs to him (Mark 12:17; Luke 20:25). The bottom line is that Christians are not only to obey public officials but also to render them honor when they serve well (1 Peter 2:13–14). In doing so, they support a God-given authority.

❖ ❖ ❖

Verses 8–14

The way Christians should conduct themselves.

3) Read Romans 13:8–10

a) Verse 8: What are we to do with our debts?

b) Verse 8: How are we to act toward others?

c) Verse 8: What do we fulfill when we do so?

d) Verse 9: What commandments are listed?

e) Verse 9: What new commandment is fulfilled by obedience?

e) Verse 10: Love is the fulfillment of what?

Paul tells how Christians are to pay their debts when they are due. Many wrongly mistake this Scripture as teaching that borrowing is wrong. God is simply stating that we should not borrow what we cannot afford to repay (Proverbs 22:7). That being said, it is always advantageous to be free of debt. While Jesus told how we should lend money to those who ask (Matthew 5:42), charging interest to believers is wrong. The Law forbids interest on loans to a countryman (Exodus 22:25; Deuteronomy 23:19; Psalm 15:5), but interest on loans to a foreigner was allowed (Deuteronomy 23:20).

Notice the commandments Paul used in verse nine and how they apply to how we treat others (Exodus 20:13–15, 17). The essential point of the four commandments is love. If we love our neighbor as ourselves, we will naturally not commit adultery, murder, steal, or even covet what they have. These commandments are only fulfilled in the law of love (John 15:17; Matthew 22:36–40).

While Christians are no longer under God's Law (Galatians 5:18), we are under a new law that was foretold in the Old Testament (John 13:34–35; Luke 10:27; Leviticus 19:18). This law can only be fulfilled by love (Matthew 7:12; Galatians 5:14) which is a fruit of the Holy Spirit (Galatians 5:22–23). James calls this the "royal law" (James 2:8), which is described as the law of Christ summarized by bearing one another's burdens (Galatians 6:2; Romans 12:15, 15:1). Know that the love we show is to also be directed toward non-believers (Matthew 5:44; Luke 6:27).

4) Read Romans 13:11–14

a) Verse 11: What other fact should motivate Christians?

b) Verse 12: What is gone and what is near?

c) Verse 12: What should this truth motivate us to do?

d) Verse 13: In light of this truth, how are we to act?

e) Verse 13: What six things are we instructed to avoid?

f) Verse 13: What are we instructed to do instead?

g) Verse 14: How are we to treat our flesh?

Paul now tells how Christians should live their lives with an eternal perspective. Notice how he also exhorts us to wake up from sleep. Why? Because Christians can be awake yet spiritually asleep, not aware of the schemes of the devil or the opportunities we have been given to glorify Jesus (2 Corinthians 2:11; Ephesians 6:11). We are exhorted to be sober and alert (1 Thessalonians 5:6; 1 Peter 5:8) because no matter your age, your life is like a vapor (Job 7:7; Psalm 39:5, 144:4; James 4:14).

Who knows the day when their own death is near (Luke 12:19–20)? Christians should live their lives knowing that the day of our salvation becomes nearer every day (James 5:8; 1 Peter 4:7). This is one reason we should not forsake assembling together (Hebrews 10:25), a time when we encourage each other to praise Him who has called us out of the darkness and promised us eternal life. The blessings we have been given by our Lord (1 Corinthians 2:9) should be enough to motivate us to serve Him all the more (2 Corinthians 5:14).

While we are encouraged that Jesus paid the penalty of death for our sins (Romans 8:1), all Christians will have to stand before the bema judgment seat of Christ (2 Corinthians 5:10), where we will give an account as to how we served Him with the gifts we have been given (Luke 19:15–26). The little time we have left on this earth should be spent developing our relationship with the Lord (Matthew 25:13; Deuteronomy 4:29) and serving Him in a way that will store up treasures in Heaven (Matthew 6:20; 1 Timothy 6:17–19). Offering ourselves daily to Him is the first step to helping accomplish this goal (Romans 12:1).

While Christians will not be judged concerning salvation (John 3:18), all non-believers will have to participate in the White Throne judgment, which happens after the millennium (Revelation 20:12–13). Christians formerly lived in a world overcome by darkness (Colossians 1:13) but were moved to the light of the kingdom of God (John 12:46; Acts 26:18). Since all Christians are sons of light (Ephesians 5:8), Paul exhorts us to be watchful and self-controlled by staying awake, alert (1 Corinthians 16:13; Ephesians 6:18), and sober (1 Peter 1:13, 5:8). This is accomplished by living an obedient life and knowing God's Word which is light (Psalm 119:105; 1 John 1:5).

While our citizenship is now in Heaven (Philippians 3:20), we presently live on this earth as ambassadors representing Jesus Christ (2 Corinthians 5:20). The result is living a life that does not include giving in to our fleshy desires as we formerly did (Galatians 5:19–20; Ephesians 2:3). Notice how all of the sins Paul mentioned result from desires of the flesh.

How do we resist the flesh? By reckoning ourselves as dead to sin (Romans 6:13), putting on the armor of light (which empowers us to stand firm against the devil) (Ephesians 6:11), and fleeing and abstaining from our lusts (2 Timothy 2:22; 1 Peter 2:11). This is also described as walking by the Spirit (Galatians 5:16). Know that fasting can help to accomplish this because abstaining from food can put the flesh into subjection to the spirit.

The way Christians should conduct themselves is summarized by telling us to put on the armor of light, which is the same as putting on the Lord Jesus. This equates to deliberate action and could be described as being kind, humble, gentle, patient, forgiving, and loving (Colossians 3:12–14), attitudes which are the same character traits of our Lord (Exodus 34:6; Numbers 14:18).

CHAPTER FOURTEEN

How Christians should treat their weaker brethren.

Verses 1–13

The way mature Christians should treat their weaker brethren.

1) Read Romans 14:1–3

a) Verse 1: What are we told to do?

b) Verses 1 & 2: What are we told not to do?

c) Verse 2: What example of a nonessential conviction does Paul use?

d) Verse 3: Should these types of issues come between believers?

Paul begins this chapter by discussing the things that can cause divisions in the church. He earlier stated that each Christian has a different measure of faith (Romans 12:3). This is why Christians are instructed to accept those weak in faith and not pass judgment on their opinions (1 Thessalonians 5:14).

How does one accept those who are weak in faith? One way is by not making someone's spiritual maturity a prerequisite for fellowship. Another is to show humility by bearing the burdens of others (Galatians 6:2). Keep in mind that most, if not all, Christians were at one time weak in faith.

While we can certainly discuss them, it is imperative not to look down on, judge, or argue with another believer about minor doctrinal issues. All Christians need to be gentle (Philippians 4:5; James 3:17), using God's Word as the final authority in any dispute (2 Timothy 3:15–17). Paul uses the example of eating specific foods. Before we continue, ask yourself this question. Is my relationship with God based on whether I eat or don't eat specific foods? The good news is we don't have to wonder as He specifically answers that question (Colossians 2:16; 1 Timothy 4:5–5).

When Paul wrote this letter, there would have been both Gentile and Jewish believers in the church in Rome. While the Gentiles would have had little or no exposure to the Law, they would have been familiar with idols. They would have also had to deal with less mature Gentile believers who might have had an issue with them eating meat that had been sacrificed to idols (1 Corinthians 8:7–13). Notice how Paul describes the one who does not eat meat as the weaker brother in the Lord. This is because Christians have been given liberty with responsibility (1 Corinthians 8:9).

Realize that, contrary to what those who practice it believe, legalism always equals weakness. Let me repeat this: Legalism equals weakness! That being said, we must again emphasize that our liberty in Christ is not a license to sin (Romans 6:15). Many of the Christian Jews would have been raised in a legalistic environment. While the more mature would have known that Christians are free from God's Law (Galatians 5:18), there would have been other Jewish believers still zealous for the Law (Acts 21:20). There was the issue of some Jews trying to place Gentile believers back under the Law, something which had been initially dealt with officially by the Church about seven or eight years before the writing of this letter (Acts 15:1–11).

2) Read Romans 14:4–6

a) Verse 4: Who alone enables believers to stand?

b) Verse 5: What is another issue besides food that can come between believers?

c) Verse 6: Whom are we living for?

We are told not to judge one another because all believers share the same righteousness (Romans 5:17; 2 Corinthians 5:21). None of us is another's master since all Christians serve Jesus alone. Keep in mind that Paul's goal was the unity of believers. This is why we have instructions on how to handle a doctrinal dispute with a weaker brother in the Lord. While God's Word is to be used (2 Timothy 3:16), we should not be judgmental in the way we present the truth.

While Paul is only discussing how we are to act concerning a nonessential doctrinal truth, we are never to waver when discussing truths such as the deity of Jesus (Philippians 2:6–7; Titus 2:13), the Holy Spirit (2 Corinthians 3:17), justification by faith alone (Romans 3:26, 5:17–18), the forgiveness of sins (Acts 13:38; Ephesians 1:9), and eternal life for all those who believe (John 3:16; 1 John 2:25). Yet even in maintaining steadfast faith we can ask God for the grace to speak the truth in love (Ephesians 4:15).

Isn't it interesting that Paul used the example of eating certain foods while the Catholic Church today forbids eating meat on certain days? Know that this heretical teaching is in direct opposition to what the Bible teaches (Acts 10:13–15; 1 Timothy 4:3), telling us that no one is to act as our judge concerning foods or holy days because this kind of doctrine which religion deems to have value is, in fact, worthless (Colossians 2:16–23).

Does disagreeing with heretical religious doctrines disobey the instruction we are given by Paul regarding judgmentalism (Romans 14:3–4)? The answer is not when discussing an essential truth, and this line is crossed with the teaching that disobedience affects your right standing with the Lord. The Catholic Church does this by insisting that disobedience to Catholic laws (not God's) is a mortal sin that will prevent one from obtaining eternal life (Catechism 2181, 2192).

Paul says that observing "special days" was another issue. Even today, there are so-called Christian groups who insist that one must obey the Sabbath and abstain from certain foods. The Catholic Church has "holy days of obligation." This is also in direct opposition to what the Word of God teaches (Galatians 4:9–11; Colossians 2:16). The bottom line is that what we eat or what days we celebrate have no bearing on our relationship with the Lord (1 Corinthians 8:8; Romans 4:17; Acts 15:11), and we are not to judge these issues unless they cross the line of declaring disobedience as a sin that affects one's relationship with Jesus. We must always hold fast to the truth of God's Word, which states that in no way is any believer superior to another. We are all sinners saved by grace, and everything we do should be for the glory of Jesus.

3) Read Romans 14:7–9

a) Verse 7: Whom are we not to live for?

b) Verse 8: Whom should we be living for?

c) Verse 8: Why?

d) Verse 9: What fact are we reminded of?

Because Christians are described as bondservants (Galatians 1:10) and enslaved to God (Romans 6:22), we should be living our lives for His glory alone, but what prevents us from doing so? Giving in to the desires of our flesh (Galatians 5:16; Ephesians 2:3; 1 John 2:16) or being distracted by the world. Those who do so are disobedient to God's command that we be separate from the world (2 Corinthians 6:17).

Many times, Christians and even leaders can make the mistake of fearing man rather than God (Deuteronomy 1:17; Proverbs 29:25). This was exemplified by the Apostle Peter, who, after being shown the truth by the Lord (Acts 10:9–15), still had to be rebuked by Paul for trying to please the Jews (Galatians 2:11–14). Notice how Paul uses the word "Lord" seven times in verses 5 to 9, strongly implying the place that Jesus should have in the life of all Christians.

How do we live for God alone? By first confessing Jesus as Lord (Romans 10:9), then living for His glory (2 Corinthians 5:15; 1 Corinthians 6:20; Philippians 2:10–11). We should intentionally live our lives to please Him (Romans 12:1; Ephesians 5:10), also remembering that we have been purchased with His blood (Acts 20:28) and are slaves to righteousness (Romans 6:19, 22).

We are again shown the importance of not only the death (2 Corinthians 5:14–15) but also the resurrection of Jesus (Romans 6:4). We have been crucified with Christ (Galatians 2:20) and now belong to Him (Galatians 5:24). Christians are a new creation due to the fact they have been baptized into Christ's death and resurrection (2 Corinthians 5:17). The result is Jesus being Lord over both the dead and the living.

4) Read Romans 14:10–13

a) Verses 10 & 13: What are we again told not to do?

b) Verses 11 & 12: Why?

c) Verse 13: What are we told not to put in a brother's way?

No matter where or how we live our lives, we should do so for the Lord, not to judge or critique the lives of our fellow Christians (Matthew 7:1; Luke 18:9–14). Paul tells how both the weak and strong in faith can be guilty of judging each other, forgetting there is only one judge (Psalm 50:6; Acts 10:42, 17:31), and all Christians will face judgment before Him (James 4:12).

God has called His children to be separate but not naive concerning spiritual matters (2 Corinthians 6:7). He wants us to know the difference between truth and error, right and wrong. That being said, the context of these verses involves personal convictions. Things Christians wrongly judge each other for include outward appearance and petty things like dancing, going to the movies, smoking cigarettes or cigars, watching television, celebrating Halloween, and playing cards (John 7:24; James 2:1–4).

Isn't it amazing how Satan can use these trivial things to divide believers? Remember there will be no finger-pointing at the time of our judgment (2 Corinthians 5:10). We will only have to answer to Jesus, who will judge both the living and the dead (2 Timothy 4:1). All Christians will give an account as to whether our lives were pleasing to Him (1 Corinthians 3:13–15; 1 Peter 4:5; Matthew 12:46). All non-Christians will bow before Jesus at the White Throne judgment where they will be told of their eternal fate for rejecting Him (Isaiah 45:23; Philippians 2:10; Revelation 20:11–15).

A natural question, then, is: Should Christians judge anything? Yes, but while God tells us to judge certain things, we should never judge the motives of another. Scripture tells us to judge only those within the Church, and any judgment should never include condemnation (Matthew 7:15; 1 Corinthians 5:12–15). Let me repeat that Christians are never to judge concerning the identity of real believers.

There are, however, things that Christians are encouraged to do that include judgment. This would be exemplified by being told not to associate with a so-called believer who is not living his or her life in a way that honors the Lord (1 Corinthians 5:11), judging the accuracy of what we are being taught (Acts 17:11; 1 John 4:1), disputes between believers (1 Corinthians 6:1-8), and also when appointing potential elders and deacons (1 Timothy 3:1–4; Titus 1:5–9) who if caught in sin are to be publicly rebuked (1 Timothy 5:20).

There are times when church leaders might have to determine whether a woman is dressed too provocatively for a church service (1 Timothy 2:9). Christians also have to determine whether a potential business partner or spouse is who they say they are (2 Corinthians 6:14–15). Paul even encourages Christians to discern good and evil (Hebrews 5:14), expose the deeds of darkness (Ephesians 5:11), and watch out and avoid those who cause divisions in the church (Romans 16:17).

God tells us it is better to focus on not letting our brother or sister stumble than judging them. Jesus' statement in Matthew 7:1, "Judge not, that you be not judged," is often quoted out of context as an absolute prohibition against all judgments. But the context helps us see that Jesus intended us to judge wisely with a continual guideline of treating others as we want to be treated, even when others see errors in our lives.

In Paul's teaching, we are told how the maturity of one's faith, which can be exemplified by eating all foods and freedom from observing any day, should not be a stumbling block for our weaker brethren. We should not flaunt our freedom in front of either non-believers or even weak Christians, as the result can be a greater temptation to sin (1 Corinthians 8:9). For instance, a Christian should not drink wine around someone who struggles with alcohol, as they might misinterpret our freedom as a license to sin. Paul instructs Christians to help our weaker brethren and not judge them. We should keep in mind that while everything is lawful (1 Corinthians 10:23–24), it is not necessarily profitable for the good of our neighbors whom we are to love as ourselves (Galatians 5:14; James 2:8).

Verses 14–23

The evil of offending our brother.

5) Read Romans 14:14–17

a) Verse 14: What truth are we told?

b) Verse 14: Even with this truth, what warning are we given?

c) Verse 15: How can our freedom affect a weaker brother?

d) Verse 15: What are we not walking in if we cause our brother to fall?

e) Verse 15: What can misusing our freedom do?

f) Verse 16: What exhortation are we given?

g) Verse 17: What does the kingdom of God have to do with things of the flesh?

h) Verse 17: How is the kingdom of God described?

Even though Jesus declared all foods to be clean (Mark 7:15–19; Acts 10:9–15), many believing Jews and Gentiles in the early church must have struggled to get freedom from the religious tradition they were taught. While man should use God's Word to determine how he lives, the real fact is the conscience of many is weak and can be negatively influenced by the actions of others (1 Corinthians 8:10). Thus, we are not to do anything that could cause a spiritual problem for a brother in the Lord, as by intentionally doing so we are sinning against Christ (1 Corinthians 8:7–13).

Realize that even if a believer is wrong, going against his conscience is something he should not do, as the guilt he experiences can and will defile him. For instance, if someone believes that going to a movie is a sin and then chooses to go, they will feel unmerited guilt that the enemy may use to drive them from God. I experienced this guilt when missing mass on a holy day of obligation or if I ate meat on Friday. I would turn away from the Lord, thinking I was condemned for doing things that were not even sin. This is why one must not exceed what is written (1 Corinthians 4:6). Remember that only God's Word has the authority to define sin.

Paul closed the issue of meat being offered to idols by exhorting the readers to eat any meat set before them and without asking questions (1 Corinthians 10:25–28), but not to eat if told that it was sacrificed to idols. Christians should not allow their liberty to cause anyone to stumble. Remember, love should always be the motivating factor in our lives (Ephesians 5:2).

We are told how we should conduct ourselves with less mature Christians. We should never allow our freedom in Christ to be spoken of as evil. God is interested in our hearts and how we treat others (1 Corinthians 12:26), not in what we do or don't eat. We are told how the things of the flesh should not be the focus of one's life but rather those of the spirit (Romans 8:6), which are righteousness, peace, and joy (Galatians 5:22).

It is ridiculous how Christians allow insignificant things to come between them. God's Word tells us that Christianity is not about eating, drinking, or celebrating certain days or feasts but rather freedom from sin, along with peace and joy in the Holy Spirit. Instead of focusing on the shortcomings of other brothers or sisters in the Lord, we should be rejoicing in the eternal life we have been given and how we can better serve our Lord.

God warns that religious (man-made) doctrines can take you captive (Colossians 2:8, 16–17) and, while they seem to have value, are, in fact, worthless (Colossians 2:23). Know they cannot deliver the needed perfection for eternal life that is only available by faith (Hebrews 9:9–10; Romans 3:28, 5:1).

6) Read Romans 14:18–20

a) Verse 18: What are we told about those who obey?

b) Verse 19: What two things are we to pursue?

c) Verse 20: What can the wrong actions do?

d) Verse 20: How does God balance the truth that all things are clean?

Paul reminds us how we serve Christ in all of life. This is something many of us fail to fully realize. Knowing that while our acceptance by God has nothing to do with our works (Romans 11:6), we should live our life trying to please and glorify Him and not man (1 Thessalonians 4:1).

Take a moment and ask yourself these questions:

• Am I living my life in a way that pleases Jesus?

• Am I taking advantage of my freedom in a way that might negatively affect another believer or non-believer?

Jesus taught us that our works should shine before men, causing them to glorify the Father (Matthew 5:16). This should be the goal of all Christians. This means we should live our lives not doing anything that could cause our brother to stumble or create a barrier for non-believers who are constantly watching (1 Peter 2:12; 2 Timothy 2:22).

One way this is accomplished is to pursue peace (Romans 14:19; Ephesians 4:29), which results in others being edified (1 Corinthians 10:23). The common goal of all Christians should be a greater maturity in the Lord. While this is an individual responsibility, we should not tear down but rather encourage each other (1 Thessalonians 5:11–14; Hebrews 3:13) in the truths of the Lord (1 Peter 2:2, 3:18), with the ultimate goal being our spiritual growth (Ephesians 4:15).

Contrast this truth with the fact that we are told how it is evil to misuse our freedom in a way that tears down the work of God. The key point is that God is at work in all Christians (1 Corinthians 12:6, 15:10; Philippians 2:13). Because of that fact, Christians should not allow non-essential truths to tear down the body of Christ. Trivial things like types of worship music, dress codes, and service times or days have caused unnecessary divisions within churches. Simply putting others ahead of ourselves would eliminate most problems.

7) Read Romans 14:21–23

a) Verse 21: What is good not to do?

b) Verse 22: How are we to use our faith?

c) Verse 22: What will keep us contented?

d) Verse 23: What about those who cause one to stumble?

e) Verse 23: Why?

f) Verse 23: What about one who goes against his conscience?

We are instructed to give preference to those weaker in faith. While drinking wine itself is not wrong (1 Timothy 5:23), one should not cause one who struggles with alcohol to stumble by flaunting our freedom. One should also not drink wine around other believers who think it wrong. Doing this equates to sacrificing our desires for the sake of our weaker brothers (1 Corinthians 8:13). Notice how God states that the one who is strong in faith will have peace, knowing that their standing with God is not affected by whether they eat or drink. With that being said, Christians are exhorted to keep their strong convictions between themselves and God; that is, don't force their opinions on others. Using our freedom in private is between us and God, while using our freedom in public is between us, God, and our brother.

Incorrectly using our freedom in Christ can cause a brother to stumble and also condemn us. We are told that when one weak in faith goes against their conscience, they can expect to be condemned by it (1 John 3:21). Even though all foods are clean (Romans 14:14), forcing an immature believer to eat meat sacrificed to idols could cause them great harm spiritually. Paul reiterates the importance of faith while telling believers how the Christian life is defined by faith (Hebrews 11:6).

One must not mistake this chapter as condoning a gospel that places people back under the Law. Remember that any doctrine that teaches that righteousness is somehow attained by observing days and abstaining from certain foods is a false gospel (Galatians 1:6–8). God plainly states that these things might appear to have value but are, in fact, both weak (Galatians 4:9–10) and worthless (Colossians 2:20–23). Anyone seeking justification through these things needs to be lovingly and patiently shown the error of their ways (Galatians 5:4).

CHAPTER FIFTEEN

*Just as Jesus did, Christians should put
their brothers ahead of themselves.*

◆ ◆ ◆

Verses 1–7

Christians should put the welfare of others ahead of themselves.

1) Read Romans 15:1–4

a) Verse 1: What are the strong instructed to do?

b) Verses 1 & 2: How can we do this?

c) Verse 2: Who are we to put first?

d) Verse 3: Who is our example?

e) Verse 3: What Scripture does Paul quote?

f) Verse 4: What does Paul remind us about concerning the Old Testament Scriptures?

g) Verse 4: What are we to learn from them?

h) Verse 4: What will the result be?

Paul now tells how we are not only not to judge others (Romans 14:1) but also to bear the burdens of our brethren in the Lord (Galatians 6:2; 1 Thessalonians 5:14). This normally involves sacrifice. One way to do this is to live by putting others first (1 Corinthians 10:24; Philippians 2:3–4). As we previously discussed, another way is to accept those weaker in faith and not use our liberty in a way that will cause others to stumble. The bottom line is that the common goal of all Christians should be building the Body of Christ (Romans 14:19), which includes all of our brothers and sisters in the Lord.

Paul earlier emphasized the insignificance of sacrificing things like food and drink (Romans 14:21). He now tells how Jesus exemplified the ultimate sacrifice by coming to this earth (Psalm 69:7–8; Philippians 2:7) to fulfill His Father's will (John 4:34, 5:30, 6:38). In doing so, He gave Himself up for everyone (Galatians 1:4; Ephesians 5:2; Titus 2:14). We are reminded that any sacrifice we make for the sake of the body of Christ cannot be compared with the sacrifice Jesus made for us.

We are told that all Scripture is inspired by God and useful for training (2 Timothy 3:16). This, of course, includes the Old Testament which was written for our instruction (1 Corinthians 10:11). Paul applies this truth by quoting David concerning the zeal Jesus had for the temple (Psalm 69:9). The instruction we should take from this is that all Christians should have the same zeal for the spiritual temple of God (1 Corinthians 3:16–17). This is only accomplished by putting the greater need of the Body of Christ ahead of our own needs (Mark 10:42–45), being devoted to each other (Romans 12:10), not arrogant (Romans 12:3), loving each other as ourselves (Romans 13:8), and by not judging one another (Romans 14:1).

2) Read Romans 15:5–7

a) Verse 5: What two gifts does God give through the Scriptures?

b) Verse 5: What do they give us?

c) Verse 5: What will they grant us to be?

d) Verse 6: What will this allow us to do?

e) Verse 7: What are we again instructed to do?

f) Verse 7: What truth should encourage us to do this?

Paul describes his prayer for those in Rome, hoping that God would give them the same mind and one voice. Remember that it is through His Word that God gives us both perseverance and encouragement so that we can use them to bring unity to the Body of Christ (Psalm 133:1; John 17:23). The key is reading Scripture, which results in us being like-minded, which is necessary for unity. We are once again shown the importance of using God's Word in church services. It is difficult for believers gathered for worship to glorify God unless they are unified.

Reading the Old Testament should encourage Christians to persevere (Romans 15:4) as it reveals God's faithfulness to His many promises (Numbers 23:19; Psalm 119:140). One of the blessings revealed is that God keeps His Word despite our unfaithfulness (Romans 3:3; 2 Timothy 2:13). Christians can count on the fact that all the promises of God are always "yes" in Jesus (Hebrews 10:23; 2 Corinthians 1:20).

When the apostles were faced with disputes concerning the serving of food (Acts 6:1–3), they recognized that serving spiritual food was much more important (John 6:27), but they found a wise way to meet the less significant need. Many fail to realize the importance of the unity of Christians (Ephesians 4:3), which can only be found in the maturity that reading and studying Scripture brings (Ephesians 4:13–14; Hebrews 6:1). We must remember the Christian life should be centered on the Word of God which performs its work in us (1 Thessalonians 2:13).

The goal of spiritual maturity is to unite all Christians in their praise of the Almighty God. This should result in not disagreeing over simple, insignificant issues that the world watches and takes pleasure in (1 Corinthians 4:9). Know that when disputes do happen, God's Word alone is to be used as the final authority (2 Timothy 3:16–17). Ignorance of Scripture is the devil's best ally.

Just as Jesus has accepted us as we are, Christians are to accept and not judge others whom the Lord has called (Romans 14:14) and purchased with His blood (Acts 20:28). This should be easier when we realize how Jesus predestined all Christians (Romans 8:29) before they were even born and our calling is something we had nothing to do with (Romans 9:11, 16; Deuteronomy 7:7). Know God did not choose us because we were good, merciful, or in any way worthy of this calling.

Verses 8–13

Jesus became a servant for the salvation of both the Jews and Gentiles.

3) Read Romans 15:8–13

a) Verse 8: What did Jesus do?

b) Verse 8: What did this fulfill?

c) Verse 9: Who else did Jesus come for?

d) Verses 9-12: What will the Gentiles do and why?

e) Verse 13: How is God described?

f) Verse 13: What does He fill you with?

g) Verse 13: What will this enable us to do?

h) Verse 13: With the help of Whom?

While Jesus initially came to this earth to serve the Jews (Matthew 10:5–6, 15:24), He also ministered to Gentiles (Matthew 8:5–13, 15:22-28; Luke 2:32). He emptied Himself (Philippians 2:7) because it was His Father's plan from all of eternity (2 Timothy 1:9). This also confirmed the promises that were made to Abraham (Genesis 22:18), Isaac (Genesis 26:4) and Jacob (Genesis 28:14). In fact, Jesus fulfilled over four hundred prophecies concerning Himself, many of which told how He came not only for the Jews but also the Gentiles (2 Samuel 22:50; Romans 3:29).

We know that salvation (Romans 11:30) has come to the Gentiles (Deuteronomy 32:43; Isaiah 11:10; Psalm 117:1), who, together with the Jews, will glorify God for His mercy (Acts 13:46–48). Paul quotes David, who told how the faithfulness of God would result in Gentiles praising Him among all the nations (Psalm 18:49). Paul stresses this to ensure that neither the Jews nor the Gentiles would look down on each other.

How did the gospel first come? Through the Jews (John 4:22). Remember, Paul was a Jewish evangelist sent to the Gentiles (Acts 22:21; Galatians 1:16, 2:7; Ephesians 3:8). In the Body of Christ, God does not differentiate between Jew and Gentile. When someone gets saved, He sends His Spirit within that individual (Romans 8:9–11; Colossians 1:27) as a down payment on their salvation (Ephesians 1:14). Many fail to realize that this is just the beginning of the Christian life, for we must all remember that God is faithful to complete the work He has begun in us (Philippians 1:6, 2:13).

Every good thing we have is a gift from God (James 1:17). This includes the grace we need (Hebrews 4:16) along with the fruits of the Spirit which result from God working in us (Galatians 5:22). Things like our hope in God (1 Timothy 4:10), joy (Acts 13:52), and peace (Romans 4:17) are all results of the indwelling Spirit (Ezekiel 36:27–28). God fills us with hope through the gift of faith, which allows us to believe (Ephesians 2:8–9).

❖ ❖ ❖

Verse 14–19

Paul modestly tells of his past work for the Lord and the nature of his ministry.

4) Read Romans 15:14–16

a) Verse 14: What should Christians be able to do for one another?

b) Verse 15: How did Paul stress this?

c) Verse 15: What gave Paul the authority to teach so boldly?

d) Verse 16: What did Paul state that his mission was?

e) Verse 16: How is this office described?

f) Verse 16: How is the Trinity involved in the ministry of the gospel?

While Paul had not yet visited the Church at Rome (Romans 1:10, 15:22) but had criticized their divisions over trivial matters, he must have heard of their spiritual maturity which allowed them to use the Word to instruct and encourage other brothers and sisters in the Lord (1 Thessalonians 5:14; Proverbs 27:17; Colossians 1:28, 3:16). The goodness he noted was a fruit of the Spirit they had (Galatians 5:22), which was a result of not only knowing God's Word but also applying it in their lives. Realize it is not good to instruct others unless you are also obeying God (James 3:1).

Notice how Paul made sure that the important points he made in this letter were written boldly. This would serve to remind them of things they already knew (2 Peter 1:12; Jude 1:5). While our spiritual disciplines should include both prayer and studying the Word (1 Thessalonians 5:17; 2 Timothy 2:15), we should also have regular times of reviewing what we have already learned. It should never be taken for granted that a fellow Christian has the proper foundation of Biblical doctrines. This is a mistake that many Christian churches make.

Leaders have the responsibility to shepherd the flock into what is good for them. That, of course, includes encouraging the reading and applying of God's Word, which is the spiritual food He has given to everyone (Deuteronomy 8:3; John 6:48). Reading God's Word cleanses (Ephesians 5:26), that is, it removes the dirt we accumulate in our minds. God's Word is the light that He uses to illuminate the path of His will (Psalm 43:3, 119:05). I believe this is why challenging Bible studies are so important.

Paul talks of the grace given to him, which he knew empowered his ministry. Notice how he described himself as a priest of the gospel of Jesus. Realize that, unlike what the present church in Rome teaches, this term is not designated to a select few but applies to all Christians (1 Peter 2:5–9; Revelation 1:6, 5:10). All Christians are priests. Therefore, we have a responsibility to give the gospel to all, with the result being that those who receive it come to God. The Levitical priesthood passed with the death of Jesus. This fact was revealed with the veil of the Temple being torn (Matthew 27:51), showing that all have access to God, previously limited to only the Jewish High Priest (Ephesians 3:11).

What were the responsibilities of the Levitical priests? They ministered in the sanctuary, offering sacrifices, taught the people the Law, and inquired of the Lord for the people concerning His will.

These are things that Christians now do. Let me repeat this: These are things that Christians now do. Under the New Covenant there is no need for sacrifices as we are told to offer our bodies as living sacrifices (Romans 12:1) and offer a sacrifice of praise (Hebrews 13:15). As for teaching the people, God's Word is very clear that while there are those called to be pastors and teachers (Ephesians 4:11), the indwelling Spirit is ultimately our teacher (John 14:26; 1 John 2:27). As to knowing God's will, Christians can go directly to Him for the answer (James 1:5). That being said, you can understand why the formal priesthood passed after the death and resurrection of Jesus.

Under the Old Covenant, the priesthood wasn't something you attained; rather, it was a birthright. One was born into the tribe of Levi, specifically a descendant of Aaron (Exodus 28:1, 29:9). This was an analogy of what was to come as being a New Covenant priest is also a birthright due to the fact that it is simply a gift from the Lord, a birthright, predestined from the beginning of time (Romans 8:28) for all who become children of God (John 1:12).

God's will in the life of Paul was for him to be the apostle to the Gentiles (Galatians 2:8–9; Ephesians 3:8). In describing his role, Paul again shows the importance of the gospel as ministering it with the empowerment of the Holy Spirit (Romans 10:17) is what qualifies Christians, using the righteousness of Jesus Christ that makes them acceptable to the Father (1 Corinthians 1:30, 6:11; Romans 8:30). Notice the role of the Trinity in ministering the gospel. Paul called himself a minister of Jesus (Romans 1:1), of the gospel of the Father (John 3:16), empowered by the Holy Spirit.

Notice how Paul considered this his priestly duty, which fulfills Isaiah's prophecy that Jews would bring Gentiles before God as an offering (Isaiah 66:20). Again, he used the gospel, which was presented to the Gentiles, who were then converted, sanctified by the Holy Spirit, and offered to God as a living sacrifice. By the time this letter was written, Paul's ministry had spanned a period of about twenty-three years.

Contrary to what many teach or believe, God has a specific will for your life (Jeremiah 10:23, 29:11; Proverbs 16:9; Romans 1:9–11), which He freely reveals to those who seek it (Matthew 6:10). The fact that God's Word tells us to pray for the knowledge of His will shows that there are times His specific will is not always revealed in His Word (Colossians 1:9). Offering ourselves to God is an important step to obtaining this knowledge (Psalm 37:4, Psalm 32:8).

We are given an example of how Christians are to live by how the Holy Spirit interacted with the Jews in the wilderness. When His presence in the pillar of cloud and fire moved out (Numbers 9:17–19), the Jews followed. When He stayed, the Jews stayed camped. Christians have the advantage of the same Spirit who both indwells and leads them.

5) Read Romans 15:17–19

a) Verse 17: How did Paul's accomplishments appear to give him grounds to boast?

b) Verse 18: What did Paul decide to do instead?

c) Verse 18: What did Christ's work result in?

d) Verse 19: What bore witness to the working of Christ?

While the fruit of the Gentiles gave him reason to boast, Paul explained elsewhere that he could and would not boast in anything (Jeremiah 9:24; 1 Corinthians 1:31) except what the Lord had done through him (Acts 15:12, 21:19; 2 Corinthians 3:5). Notice how the result was obedience from the Gentiles which is a sure sign of salvation (Acts 17:30; 1 Peter 1:2). Know that bearing fruit brings much glory to the Lord (John 15:8; Colossians 1:18).

While Paul performed miracles such as raising Eutychus from the dead (Acts 20:9-12), he also suffered many trials (2 Corinthians 11:23–27). Realize that miracles only bear witness to the truth being proclaimed (Hebrews 2:4), as it is the gospel that does the work (Acts 19:20; Romans 1:16; 1 Corinthians 1:18). This truth is exemplified when after witnessing the raising of Lazarus from the dead (John 11:43–53), the priests and Pharisees did not believe but rather decided to kill Jesus. It was also exemplified when the Lord used Paul to heal a man at Lystra who had been lame from birth (Acts 14:8–10). The response of the people was not to believe in the gospel of Jesus Christ but rather to stone Paul (Acts 14:19).

While we are told how Paul's great ministry covered an area of almost fifteen hundred miles across (Jerusalem to Illyricum), God's Word gives no account of Paul's ministry in Illyricum (modern-day Baltic states of Albania, Serbia, and Bosnia). The Lord kept Paul humble by giving him a thorn in the flesh, which would keep him from exalting himself (2 Corinthians 12:4–9). While many so-called Christian leaders have a high opinion of themselves, it's only the Lord's opinion that matters (John 5:30, 8:16). The Catholic Church makes a blanket statement considering its leaders (Catechism 773), "The structure of the church is totally ordered to the holiness of Christ's members." Also, priests are like the living image of God the Father (Catechism 1549).

The Lord who is slow to anger and abounding in loving kindness (Exodus 34:6), searches the hearts of men (Proverbs 15:11), being able to judge even our intentions (Hebrews 4:12). It will not be until the Judgment Day that it will be revealed who pleased the Lord with their actions (Luke 13:30).

That being said, I believe there are five reasons we should not boast in the Lord as an expression of personal pride:

I. God has chosen the weak and the foolish to shame the wise and strong. If you are doing anything great for the Lord, it is only because you were the least likely person to do it in the first place (1 Corinthians 1:27).

II. Even the works we do accomplish were predestined by God (Ephesians 2:10).

III. Christians have no strength on their own. One can only accomplish what God does through them (Acts 15:12, 21:19; 2 Corinthians 3:5).

IV. God exalts the humble and is opposed to the proud (James 4:6; 1 Peter 5:5).

V. All will have to give an account to God for their actions (Romans 14:12).

All Christians should remain humble, knowing that they have no strength in themselves. Our only hope is in the Lord (Psalm 146:5).

❖ ❖ ❖

Verses 20–28

Paul tells of his present plans.

5) Read Romans 15:20–23

a) Verse 20 & 21: What was Paul's goal in preaching the gospel?

b) Verse 22: Why had Paul not yet visited Rome?

c) Verse 23: Why did Paul now want to visit Rome?

Paul considered his mission to be to give the gospel to those who had not yet heard it. The fact that others were presenting the gospel in Rome and Paul was busy in Asia Minor prevented him from coming there, as he considered his mission to be to non-believers. He quoted Isaiah, who, while describing the Messiah's ministry at His second coming (Isaiah 52:15), also seemed to encourage Paul in his endeavors. This passage can also encourage those with the gift of evangelism.

As I previously stated, there were converts from Rome on the day of Pentecost (Acts 2:10), so there must have been a church in Rome long before Paul arrived. It seems that Paul had decided that since the gospel had been sufficiently preached in Asia Minor (Acts 19:21), he could now come to Rome.

6) Read Romans 15:24–28

a) Verse 24: What did he say about his future plans?

b) Verse 25: What city was Paul first planning on going to?

c) Verse 26: What had those in Macedonia and Achaia done?

d) Verse 27: Why?

e) Verse 27: What justification is given for this?

f) Verse 28: How did Paul describe the gift he was bringing to those in Jerusalem?

God's plans are often different from ours (Acts 16:7). While Paul had intended to go to Spain (Acts 19:21), also known as Tarshish (1 Kings 10:22), via Jerusalem and then Rome, we know that he left Corinth (where he wrote this letter), traveled via Macedonia, Philippi, Troas, Assos, Miletus, and Caesarea, and was arrested after arriving in Jerusalem (Acts 23:27).

After being held in Israel for three years, Paul was taken to Rome (around 60-61 AD) (Acts 28:14–17) where he was held under house arrest. During this time, he wrote letters to the Ephesians, Philippians, Colossians, and Philemon. About 63 AD, Paul was acquitted and released, but in 67 AD, he was again arrested and taken back to Rome, where he would write 1st and 2nd Timothy before being beheaded.

Paul was bringing a contribution to the poor Christian Jews in Jerusalem from the Gentiles in Macedonia and Achaia (1 Corinthians 16:1–3). Notice how Paul calls this their fruit. Gentiles have a responsibility to help not only their Jewish brothers and sisters in the Lord (Acts 10:1–2; 1 Corinthians 9:11; Galatians 2:10, 6:6) but also other Gentiles who shared the Word with them. This is a good example of how believers are to treat one another. It is, in fact, the least we can do for our Lord who came to this earth and became poor for us (Matthew 25:45; 2 Corinthians 8:9).

❖ ❖ ❖

Verses 29–33

Paul tells of his future plans.

7) Read Romans 15:29–33

a) Verse 29: What was Paul confident of?

b) Verse 30: What are those in Rome urged to do?

c) Verses 31 & 32: What are they to pray for?

d) Verse 33: How is God now described?

Paul asked for prayer because he knew what he would face in Jerusalem (Acts 20:22–23). He was aware of the importance and power of intercessory prayer (Colossians 1:9–12), which was modeled by Jesus, who continually makes intercession for all believers (John 17:6–26; Romans 8:34; Hebrews 7:25). Paul also wanted the Jewish believers to receive the gift with gratitude. This would be no small thing, as they typically looked down on Gentiles from whom the gifts were coming.

The Old Testament gives many examples of the power of prayer:

- Moses interceded after the spies brought back a bad report concerning the Promised Land (Numbers 14:13–20).

- Samuel prayed for the nation of Israel after they rejected God as their king (1 Samuel 12:23).

- King Hezekiah and Isaiah interceded when faced with a siege by the Assyrian King Sennacherib (Isaiah 37:4, 21–29).

- Daniel interceded regarding the time of the return of the Jews from their captivity (Daniel 9:2–20).

- Nehemiah interceded when he heard about the conditions in Jerusalem (Nehemiah 1:2–14).

Does Biblical intercession ever include prayers performed by dead saints? Absolutely not! God forbids any interaction with the dead (Leviticus 20:6; Deuteronomy 18:10–12). Saul calling on a dead Samuel for help cost him his life (1 Samuel 28; 1 Chronicles 10:13). Even the idolatrous Jews knew not to and did not pray to Abraham, Isaac, Jacob, Moses, or even Elijah or Elisha.

This fact is in direct conflict with the following Roman Catholic statements: "Saints intercede directly to the Father offering their works done while on this earth" (Catechism 956, 2683); "Prayers to saints not only help them but also make them more effective intercessors" (Catechism 958); "Saints care for those left on earth" (Catechism 2683); and "the church asks intercession from saints" (Catechism 2692).

It is interesting to note that both Peter (2 Peter 1:14) and Paul (2 Timothy 4:6) wrote how their deaths were imminent, and neither stated that they would pray for the recipients of their epistles after their death. Why not? Because they knew and believed that you don't pray to anyone but Jesus. All believers have been clothed with the righteousness of Jesus (Galatians 3:27), which now allows them to come directly into the Father's presence through Him (Ephesians 2:18, 3:12). We are in fact encouraged to do so (Ephesians 6:18).

While we can go directly to God through Jesus, God's Word is clear: There are no other intercessors between God and man (John 14:6; 1 Timothy 2:5). God is described as the God of peace (2 Corinthians 13:11; Philippians 4:9). Rejoice in the fact that Jesus alone (Ephesians 2:11–14) is the source for the peace with God that believers have (John 16:33; Acts 10:36; Romans 5:1).

CHAPTER SIXTEEN

Paul's benediction.

◆ ◆ ◆

Verses 1–16

Paul sends a greeting to those in Rome.

1) Read Romans 16:1–16

a) Verse 1: Who is commended to them?

b) Verse 2: What had she done?

c) Verse 3: Who else are they to greet?

d) Verse 4: What did they do?

e) Verses 5–15: How many additional people are they instructed to greet and for what reasons?

f) Verse 16: How were the Christians to greet one another?

Notice how there seem to be at least three home churches mentioned by Paul in this chapter (Romans 16:5, 14 & 15). Phoebe was with those who were bringing this letter from Corinth to Rome. She was a servant at the church in Cenchrea (Acts 18:18).

Priscilla and Aquila had previously lived in Rome, but they were forced to leave when Claudius expelled all Jews (Acts 18:2). They not only risked their lives to help Paul but were also mature believers, demonstrated in the way they corrected and instructed Apollos (Acts 18:26). They had also been with

Paul in Corinth and led a church in their home at Ephesus and were now doing the same thing in Rome (1 Corinthians 16:19). They evidently returned to Ephesus at the time of Paul's death (2 Timothy 4:19).

While Paul describes Andronicus and Junia as fellow prisoners, he does not give specifics as to when this happened (2 Corinthians 11:23). It seems that Andronicus and Junia were (Jews) not only related to Paul but were saved before him. Rufus could be the son of Simon of Cyrene, who helped Jesus bear the cross based on Mark's mention that Simon had two sons (Rufus and Alexander) (Mark 15:21). Their inclusion in the Gospel means they must have been well known at the time it was written. While Paul refers to the mother of Rufus as his, it is unlikely that she was his natural mother.

Notice how Paul mentions ten women in these verses (Phoebe, Prisca, Junia, Mary, Tryphena, Thyphosa, Persis, Julia, the mother of Rufus and the sister of Nereus), showing the importance of women in the ministry. Women have always had a definite role in the church (1 Corinthians 14:34–35; 1 Timothy 2:12), and they are greatly used by the Lord (Philippians 4:3).

Isn't it strange that Paul mentions thirty-six people in this chapter and yet does not mention Peter even once? I bring this up because the Catholic Church states that Peter was the Bishop in Rome from the years 32-67 AD.

If Peter had been the first Pope and was present in Rome, would it not have been disrespectful for Paul not to mention him? The real truth is that there is no Biblical evidence that Peter was ever in Rome. Christian tradition says he became the Bishop of Antioch (Syria). While one cannot with any certainty state that Peter was never in Rome, there is no biblical evidence of his ever being there.

Let us see what Scripture tells us about the location of Peter's ministry:

- Rome is mentioned nine times in the New Testament, and Peter's name is not once associated with it.

- Peter was not there in 50 AD when Claudius expelled all the Jews from Rome (Acts 18:2).

- We know travel took a long time. This is exemplified by taking Paul from the fall of 60 AD until the spring of 61 AD to get to Rome from Caesarea. And that was under the authority of Roman soldiers.

- The first 12 Chapters of Acts (church history up to about 44 AD) refer to Peter's time in Palestine and Syria.

- In 50–51 AD, Peter was in Jerusalem at the Jerusalem council (Acts 15).

- Galatians 1:15–18 tells how three years after Paul became a Christian (about 33–34 AD), he went to Jerusalem and met with Peter.

- Galatians 2:1–9 tells how, fourteen years later, he went to Jerusalem and Peter was there.

- Galatians 2:11 tells how Peter had come to Antioch.

• Peter wrote 1st and 2nd Peter, but never mentions the people in Rome. Both were primarily written to Jewish believers in Asia Minor.

• Ephesians, Philippians, Colossians, and Philemon were written by Paul from prison in Rome about 61 AD, and Paul never mentions Peter. If Peter had been in Rome, they would have certainly had some contact.

• In 67 AD, Paul was again in prison in Rome, and he does not mention Peter to Timothy in 1st or 2nd Timothy. This is the same year that the Catholic Church says Peter died in Rome.

• In 2 Timothy 4:10 (67 AD), Paul says (while in Rome) that all but Luke had deserted him. Where was Peter?

• Irenaeus was the Bishop of Lyons (178–200 AD), a disciple of Polycarp, the Bishop of Smyrna, who himself was a disciple of John the Apostle. He listed the first twelve Roman Bishops, stating that the first Bishop was Linus (appointed by Paul) and the second was Clement. Irenaeus stated that Peter only died in Rome.

• If Peter was the Bishop of Rome, what right did Paul have to send religious instructions there?

After instructing to greet over three-dozen people, Paul instructs on how to greet fellow Christians. Even today, and in many cultures, people greet each other with a kiss. Jesus chastised Simon the Pharisee for not doing so (Luke 7:45), and was betrayed by a kiss (Luke 22:48). It is interesting to note that there are five times God exhorts believers to do so (1 Corinthians 16:20; 2 Corinthians 13:12; 1 Thessalonians 5:26; 1 Peter 5:14). This kiss is described as "holy" and would be an expression of brotherly love and acceptance (1 Samuel 20:41; 2 Samuel 19:39; Acts 20:37) as well as serving to portray harmony. Today, many Christians show this affection by giving each other hugs.

Verses 17–20

Paul gives a warning about false teachers.

2) Read Romans 16:17–20

a) Verse 17: What are those at Rome warned about?

b) Verse 18: How are these described?

c) Verse 18: Whom do they deceive?

d) Verse 19: What had Paul heard about those at Rome?

e) Verse 19: What exhortation does Paul give?

f) Verse 20: What promise can all Christians count on?

Unity ends when God's Word is compromised. Christians should never tolerate heresy. In warning the Romans about those who deceive and divide, Paul also encouraged them by acknowledging their spiritual maturity. All Christians should deal with anyone who either causes dissension (Matthew 7:15) or teaches things contrary to the gospel of Jesus Christ (1 Timothy 1:3; Acts 20:28–30; Galatians 1:8).

False teachers are one of the greatest dangers a church can encounter. There are usually two reasons why these deceivers are not confronted. The first is people either not knowing or using God's Word as instructed (2 Timothy 3:16). The second is feeling inferior to those with "credentials" or "titles" failing to realize how Satan will come against us (2 Corinthians 11:14). God tells us to expose the deeds of the devil (Ephesians 5:11). Realize that disobedience will always result in division and strife.

We are also instructed to turn away from those (2 Thessalonians 3:6, 14) who are described as slaves to their appetites (Philippians 3:18–19). God warns that these heretics will be successful by using smooth and flattering speech. Television evangelists promoting the false prosperity gospel (from which only they get rich) fit this description. We are told how the deceived (who are ignorant of God's Word) are described as unsuspecting or simple. It is amazing how many Christians foolishly accept and support those who preach things contrary to the Word of God.

That being said, Paul compliments those at the Church of Rome for the way they had already handled such situations. The best way to distinguish the sheep from the goats or wheat from the tares is to know God's Word (Proverbs 14:15; Matthew 10:16) and be innocent of evil (1 Corinthians 14:20). Knowing how Satan is behind these false teachers, all Christians can take solace in the fact that he will not only be defeated but crushed by our Lord Jesus (Genesis 3:15; Revelation 20:10).

Verses 21–24

Those with Paul send their greetings.

3) Read Romans 16:21–23

a) Verse 21: How is Timothy described?

b) Verse 22: Who wrote this letter for Paul?

c) Verse 23: Who was hosting Paul?

Paul sends a greeting from Timothy, whom he had met during his second missionary journey (Acts 16:1). Paul also mentions other men who were with him at Corinth. These include Lucius (Acts 13:1), Jason (Acts 17:5), Sosipater (Acts 20:4), Gaius (Acts 19:29, 20:4; 1 Corinthians 1:14), and Erastus (Acts 19:22; 2 Timothy 4:20). We are told that it was at the home of Gaius where the church at Corinth met. Lucius might have been Luke, who authored the gospel of Luke and Acts. It was Tertius who served as a scribe for this letter from Paul.

❖ ❖ ❖

Verses 25–27

Paul's closing prayer and doxology.

4) Read Romans 16:25–27

a) Verse 25: What does God use to establish you?

b) Verse 25: How was this previously revealed?

c) Verse 26: What has now been revealed?

d) Verse 26: What happens to those who trust in the gospel?

e) Verse 27: How does Paul define God?

Paul now praises God, who can and will do anything necessary to establish His children (Ephesians 3:20; Jude 24). Notice that the gospel tells how it is God who does the establishing.

How does God establish His children? The first step to becoming a believer is hearing the gospel, which is the power God uses to deliver the faith we need (Romans 1:16, 10:17). God then sets free those who are slaves to sin and who become obedient from the heart (Romans 6:14–17). This gospel was previously witnessed by the prophets and has now been made known to all the nations (Romans 1:2; Colossians 1:26; 1 Peter 1:11). The first chapter of this study discussed this subject in great detail.

Notice how Paul describes our Lord as the only wise God. This epistle has revealed much concerning His plan for salvation through His only Son, Jesus Christ. God's plan reveals His wisdom (Romans 11:32–

33).

This concludes the study of the Book of Romans. Let this be the beginning of a closer relationship with the God of all Creation! Remember that God's Word tells us that those who seek Him with all their strength will find Him (1 Chronicles 28:9). Apply this truth by dedicating yourself to seeking Him in prayer and through His Word. It will be the most important and rewarding thing you can ever do.

PRAISE TO JESUS, AND HIM BE THE GLORY!

ABOUT THE AUTHOR

William Ciofani

William Ciofani is a Bible teacher, author, husband, and father whose journey of faith began after a series of devastating diagnoses. At his lowest, he cried out to Jesus, leading to a profound transformation and a deep hunger for God's Word. Over the years, William has witnessed God's faithfulness through miraculous answers to prayer, including God's promise to heal both him and his wife. Compelled to share what he was learning, he began writing Bible studies in the mid 1990s, starting with Romans. His ministry expanded from small groups to larger classes and international training, including Biblical Answers to Catholic Questions. He served as an elder for 14 years at his home church and as a board member for Word Partners, a ministry that specializes in training pastors worldwide. Today, William's writing and teaching, rooted in personal experience and a passion for Scripture, continues to encourage believers globally to discover the life-changing power of God's Word.

LOVED THIS STUDY?

Be the First to Know About New Releases!

Twenty Seven Books is equipping believers with Christ-centered resources for every step of the way.

Subscribe to our Twenty Seven Books newsletter and podcast *In Light Of* to stay connected and get access to additional resources such as guided Bible studies, devotionals, personal reflections, and more to help transform your journey with Jesus.

Visit www.twentysevenbooks.com/inlightof
or scan the QR code below.

ACCESS STUDY RESOURCES

www.ingramcontent.com/pod-product-compliance
Lightning Source LLC
Chambersburg PA
CBHW080413170426
43194CB00015B/2799